# KNOWLEDGE ENGINEERING
# FOR EXPERT SYSTEMS

**ELLIS HORWOOD BOOKS IN INFORMATION TECHNOLOGY**
*General Editor:* Dr JOHN M. M. PINKERTON, Principal, J. & H. Pinkerton Associates, Surrey (Consultants in Information Technology), and formerly Manager of Strategic Requirements, ICL
**EXPERT SYSTEMS IN BUSINESS: A Practical Approach**
M. BARRETT, Expertech Limited, Slough, and A. C. BEEREL, Lysia Limited, London
**ELECTRONIC DATA PROCESSING, Vols. 1 and 2\***
M. BECKER, R. HABERFELLNER and G. LIEBETRAU, Zurich, Switzerland
**EXPERT SYSTEMS: Strategic Implications and Applications**
A. C. BEEREL, Lysia Limited, London
**SOFTWARE ENGINEERING ENVIRONMENTS**
P. BRERETON, Department of Computer Science, University of Keele
**SMART CARDS: Their Principles, Practice and Applications\***
R. BRIGHT, Information Technology Strategies International Limited, Orpington, Kent
**PRACTICAL MACHINE TRANSLATION\***
D. CLARKE and U. MAGNUSSON-MURRAY, Department of Applied Computing and Mathematics, Cranfield Institute of Technology, Bedford
**KNOWLEDGE-BASED SYSTEMS: Implications for Human–Computer Interfaces**
D. CLEAL, PA Computers and Telecommunications, London, and N. HEATON, Central Computer and Telecommunications Agency, London
**KNOWLEDGE-BASED MANAGEMENT SUPPORT SYSTEMS**
G. I. DOUKIDIS, F. LAND and G. MILLER, Information Management Department, London Business School
**KNOWLEDGE ENGINEERING FOR EXPERT SYSTEMS**
M. GREENWELL, Expert Systems International, Oxford
**KNOWLEDGE-BASED EXPERT SYSTEMS IN INDUSTRY**
J. KRIZ, Head of AI Group, Brown Boveri Research Systems, Switzerland
**ARTIFICIAL INTELLIGENCE: Current Applications\***
A. MATTHEWS and J. RODDY, Aregon International Ltd., London
**INFORMATION TECHNOLOGY: An Overview\***
J. M. M. PINKERTON, J. & H. Pinkerton Associates, Esher, Surrey
**EXPERT SYSTEMS IN THE ORGANIZATION: An Introduction for Decision-makers\***
S. SAVORY, Nixdorf Computer AG, FRG
**BUILDING EXPERT SYSTEMS: Cognitive Emulation**
P. E. SLATTER, Telecomputing plc, Oxford
**SPEECH AND LANGUAGE-BASED COMMUNICATION WITH MACHINES:
Towards the Conversational Computer**
J. A. WATERWORTH and M. TALBOT, Human Factors Division, British Telecom Research Laboratories, Ipswich

\* In preparation

# KNOWLEDGE ENGINEERING FOR EXPERT SYSTEMS

MIKE GREENWELL
Independent Knowledge Engineering
and Expert Systems Consultant

ELLIS HORWOOD LIMITED
Publishers · Chichester

Halsted Press: a division of
**JOHN WILEY & SONS**
New York · Chichester · Brisbane · Toronto

First published in 1988 by
**ELLIS HORWOOD LIMITED**
Market Cross House, Cooper Street,
Chichester, West Sussex, PO19 1EB, England
*The publisher's colophon is reproduced from James Gillison's drawing of the ancient Market Cross, Chichester.*

**Distributors:**
*Australia and New Zealand:*
JACARANDA WILEY LIMITED
GPO Box 859, Brisbane, Queensland 4001, Australia
*Canada:*
JOHN WILEY & SONS CANADA LIMITED
22 Worcester Road, Rexdale, Ontario, Canada
*Europe and Africa:*
JOHN WILEY & SONS LIMITED
Baffins Lane, Chichester, West Sussex, England
*North and South America and the rest of the world:*
Halsted Press: a division of
JOHN WILEY & SONS
605 Third Avenue, New York, NY 10158, USA
*South-East Asia*
JOHN WILEY & SONS (SEA) PTE LIMITED
37 Jalan Pemimpin # 05–04
Block B, Union Industrial Building, Singapore 2057
*Indian Subcontinent*
WILEY EASTERN LIMITED
4835/24 Ansari Road
Daryaganj, New Delhi 110002, India

© 1988 M. Greenwell/Ellis Horwood Limited

**British Library Cataloguing in Publication Data**
Greenwell, Mike, *1953–*
Knowledge engineering for expert systems. —
(Ellis Horwood books in information technology).
1. Expert systems
I. Title
006.3'3

**Library of Congress CIP available**

ISBN 0–7458–0513–2 (Ellis Horwood Limited)
ISBN 0–470–21132–6 (Halsted Press)

Phototypeset in Times by Ellis Horwood Limited
Printed in Great Britain by Hartnolls, Bodmin

**COPYRIGHT NOTICE**
All Rights Reserved. No part of this publication may be reproduced, stored in a retrieval system, or transmitted, in any form or by any means, electronic, mechanical, photocopying, recording or otherwise, without the permission of Ellis Horwood Limited, Market Cross House, Cooper Street, Chichester, West Sussex, England.

# Table of contents

| | | |
|---|---|---|
| **Acknowledgements** | | 7 |
| 1 | **Introduction** | 9 |
| 2 | **The nature of expertise and knowledge acquisition** | 15 |
| 3 | **Knowledge elicitation as a social situation** | 24 |
| 4 | **Interviewing theory** | 30 |
| 5 | **Techniques for knowledge elicitation** | 44 |
| 6 | **The first interview** | 76 |
| 7 | **Planning and preparation** | 92 |
| 8 | **Knowledge analysis** | 103 |
| 9 | **Management and feasilibity** | 118 |
| 10 | **The management methodology** | 135 |
| 11 | **EMEX a case study** | 150 |
| **Glossary** | | 176 |
| **Bibliography** | | 179 |
| **Index** | | 182 |

# Acknowledgements

This is an eclectic work. I have drawn from my own experiences and from other authors in this area. As I have not always been able to find the original source of an idea I have been unable to acknowledge some of the authors directly. However, I do wish to acknowledge and give thanks to the following people whose work and ideas have influenced me and eventually led to this book: W. J. Clancey, M. D. Grover, whose early work was an inspiration to many, and Bob Wielinga and Joost Brueker of the University of Amsterdam. Their contribution to the study of knowledge acquisition has been my major influence since we were all involved on the same research contract. Many thanks to Margret Welbank for her encouragement and for her early review of the techniques. Many thanks also to those I have worked with who have influenced me, including Jonathan Killin of the KBSC, Ted Walker of ESI, from whom I learnt a great deal about building a real expert system, and finally Maureen Firlej, to whom I owe a special debt of gratitude for directing me towards knowledge acquisition back in 1984.

Many thanks to the following people for their assistance and advice during the seemingly never-ending task of writing this book: Chris Dobin, Masoud Yazdani, Alex Goodall, Louis Busuttil, Catherine Kenny, Paul Ormroyd, David Owen and the rest of the ALVEY EMEX club members for allowing me to use materials from the project.

# 1
# Introduction

Expert systems are the limousines of the computer software industry. They are scarce and expensive. In recent years a number of researchers and knowledge engineers have been concerned to develop a methodology and thereby to reduce the costs involved in developing such systems. However, expert systems will always be expensive compared to conventional data processing, but it is hoped that this book and others now available will increase the reliability and utility of such systems as well as reduce the costs. By following the methodology presented here expert systems may be cheaper to build, which would mean they would be less scarce although still expensive compared to other information technology systems.

This book is not an introductory text to expert systems. There are many such books available if that is what is required. The target audience for this book are knowledge engineers, expert systems project managers and potential experts in a prospective project. The readers of this book are expected to know the meaning of such concepts as 'forward chaining rule' or 'expert systems tool kit'. However, a glossary has been included to refresh the memory.

Expert systems at the present time come in various shapes and sizes: the large application, the prototype investigation and the home-made application. The latter is produced by an individual with some expertise which he finds easy to represent using an inexpensive shell. The author is assured that this does take place but is unable to offer any evidence to support the claim, the probable reason being that successful home-grown expert systems are a prized and commercially sensitive resource for the individual in question, rather than that people are reluctant to admit failure in this enterprise.

The prototypic investigation is the most common variety of expert system. As a functioning piece of software it usually has the status of a toy and is used by management and technical staff as a vehicle to assist the general appreciation of expert systems technology. If the system develops beyond the prototypic investigation then it achieves the status of either a major commercial software system or a major project disaster.

A commercial expert system represents a substantial development cost for the large organisation which is prepared to bear the risk. It is for the technicians and management in those organisations that this book is intended. The technicians have become known as knowledge engineers, a title which seems to demand a greater respect than computer programmer or systems analyst and has the advantage of being in common use even if it is somewhat nonsensical.

Expert system projects have a record of overshooting cost projections by an alarming margin. This is not a property of expert systems alone. Standard data processing projects have also had their failures. However, expert systems have the additional problem that, even when successful, the expected benefits are not always realised to the degree suggested by the advocates of the technology. A major problem in building expert systems is the lack of an integrated methodology for knowledge engineering and a complimentary managerial perspective. This book is one attempt to define a methodology for expert systems. The primary feature of that methodology is to control the most difficult and expensive phase of building expert systems — knowledge acquisition.

The task of obtaining knowledge, required to make expert systems function has been the least understood process in building knowledge-based systems. Indeed, some workers deny that knowledge acquisition is a major issue. This lack of interest in knowledge acquisition seems to stem from the conventional data processing background possessed by many of the workers in commercial expert systems. In recent years, however, more knowledge engineers have realised the difficulties inherent in acquiring knowledge from domain experts. Knowledge acquisition has become the major issue for knowledge engineers.

Academic criticism of early expert systems pointed to conceptual weaknesses in the knowledge-bases as a major problem. Solutions from researchers with backgrounds in psychology were largely concerned with psychological factors, which gave the task of knowledge acquisition prominence. While effort was being expended upon the knowledge acquisition/knowledge analysis stage, the commercial cutting edge of the technology was producing ever more elaborate software and hardware systems. The single user workstation and the AI tool kit or recommended programming environment became the principle tools of the knowledge engineer. Unfortunately, the principles for the acquisition and analysis of expertise lagged behind, truly a case of computer power without principles.

The expert systems industry is now entering a knowledge acquisition boom. Several books on knowledge acquisition have been published recently, training in knowledge acquisition is offered and specialist computer employment agencies are searching for candidates with knowledge acquisition skills for their clients. With all this activity it should be surprising to find that knowledge engineers are thrown into knowledge acquisition without preparation. And yet this still seems to be the case. One reason may be that knowledge acquisition looks easy. Indeed, what could be easier? — ask someone what they know, what they do, and how they do it, then plug all this into a ready-made expert system shell. In fact, one of the difficulties with knowledge acquisition is precisely this attitude. When problems arise, as they certainly will with this naive approach, the fault must be with the knowledge engineer, who seemingly is not competent at what is a very simple task.

Many of the issues concerned with knowledge acquisition fall into the domain of psychology. There has always been a close relationship between cognitive psychology and artificial intelligence. The cognitive psychologist takes an information processing perspective to mental phenomena. In artificial intelligence this is demonstrated by modelling human thought processes in a computer program. A cognitive model is not an expert system, although there are some parallels. Closer correspondence between the psychologist and the knowledge engineer is found in the identification of reasoning and problem solving strategies, memory constraints and the analysis of social situations such as the knowledge elicitation session itself. An awareness of psychology is an asset for the knowledge engineer but not as important as a detailed appreciation of programming styles relevant to the implementation of the knowledge analysis.

Knowledge engineering is that branch of the computer software industry concerned with building of expert systems. Knowledge engineering is itself composed of two separate tasks. On the one hand, there are knowledge engineers who mainly program in PROLOG or LISP. The software they build supports a particular knowledge representation, facilitating the inferencing mechanisms and providing a pathway to the user. An alternative would be to encode knowledge directly into the formalism offered by a sophisticated shell or using the facilities offered by a tool kit. Conversely, there are the knowledge engineers who spend much of their time talking to domain experts and potential users and analysing the transcripts of these conversations. Other tasks include designing the system and writing the code of which the knowledge-base consists. This second type of knowledge engineer is the primary audience for this book. That is not an invitation for the former to put this book down and concentrate on the latest work on object oriented programming. The greater the division in the labour of building expert systems, the greater the probability of communication problems which inevitably lead to a weaker final system.

Definitions should never be too rigid; the definitions with respect to knowledge engineering are developing as the principles and methodology develops. Some knowledge engineers may take issue with the definitions that appear below, Nevertheless, people require terms to be defined, however imperfectly.

**Knowledge acquisition** is the collection and analysis of information from one or more domain experts and any other sources leading to the production of a number of documents which form the basis of a functioning knowledge-base. A substantial subset of knowledge acquisition is knowledge elicitation. **Knowledge elicitation** is that area of knowledge acquisition which deals with acquiring information directly from domain experts.

Some writers on knowledge acquisition seem to be drawn into discussing the domain or a specific application, and confusing this with the knowledge engineering techniques. They make statements about the knowledge engineering which seem more properly to belong to the domain. I shall attempt to restrict this book to general knowledge engineering issues and keep references to specific domains to a minimum. However, examples from an actual expert system project will be presented in chapter 11.

Instruction in the techniques of knowledge engineering will be found in chapter 5. Impatient readers are directed to move immediately to that chapter. Management issues are documented in chapters 9 and 10. Those with a specific interest in those issues are directed to that chapter and are also reminded that good management is founded on information, so they will be expected to also read those chapters dealing with techniques.

## MODES OF EXPERT SYSTEMS

There are five major types of expert systems. The descriptions of each type are set out below for the purpose of providing background knowledge which is required for a number of planning decisions. This information should also form part of the introduction to expert systems for experts, which is given by the knowledge engineer as an ice-breaking exercise before the real work begins.

> Knowledge-based information systems
> Decision support systems
> Consultation systems
> Problem solving systems
> Coaching systems

Fig. 1.1 — Basic types of knowledge-based systems.

**Knowledge-based information systems** tend to be intelligent-front-ends for accessing large databases. The knowledge required largely consists of the categorical structure of the items in the database and the user's typical modes of interaction with the database. The system assists with enquiry but does not solve problems or perform any recognised expert tasks. The knowledge required by this type of system is generally easy to obtain. Systems builders either have the requisite knowledge or can communicate without difficulty to those who have. Generally these are not very complex systems but probably beneficial and cost-effective.

**Decision support systems** take the advisory role of the expert. The system assists the user in the decision making processes by asking questions and interpreting the answers and has a powerful role as an organisational aid to decision making. However, there is little problem solving activity performed by the system. Even so, decision support systems tend to be fairly complex and require a lot of knowledge. The financial benefits may be low considering the probable high cost of building the system.

**Consultation systems** perform the reasoning in order to produce a diagnosis or report. A major feature is the ability for the user to interrogate the system's reasoning. However, explanation features are not very advanced as yet, and a large proportion of the work load will be concerned with the explanation facilities. Emphasizing explanations in the knowledge elicitation sessions will increase the potential power of the explanation facility. Financial gain may not be realised in this category of expert systems if only because the failure rate of consultation system projects is so high.

**Problem solving systems** reason and offer a diagnosis with optional advice. Some problem solvers are not knowledge-based but fall within the category of artificial intelligence solutions. If the system is knowledge-based the knowledge engineer will need to acquire vast amounts of knowledge to reach some sort of performance parity with the expert. They are complex systems which run the risk of cracking under the weight of their own complexity. They can make or save a fortune for the organisation with the sophisticated hardware and software to develop and run the finished system.

**Coaching systems** are used to coach a student through the problem solving process. A feature of this type of expert system is the ability to adapt to individual users. The knowledge-base for a coaching system is probably not very large and may well consist of scripts which the user navigates through.

## AUTOMATIC ELICITATION TECHNIQUES

In recent years there has been some work on the development of automatic systems for knowledge elicitation. This endeavour to replace the knowledge engineer by a computer program has been motivated by the difficulty and cost in eliciting knowledge. One of the reasons knowledge elicitation is so difficult and expensive is that approaches to it have been naive and unstructured. In such a situation programmatic simulations of knowledge elicitation have had to rely on procedures which were available to the programmer and possibly not used by the knowledge engineer. Three main thrusts seem to predominate: induction, reparatory grids, and documentation systems.

All three approaches have produced little in the way of useful tools for two main reasons. Firstly, the various knowledge representation languages and environments are usually incompatible with one another, so that a knowledge acquisition tool is usually dependent upon a particular environment which restricts the market for such a product. Secondly, the inferential power of these systems is particularly suspect and lacks the taken-for-granted common sense which is inherent in intelligent humans as they come to understand the expert's task and domain.

Knowledge engineering documentation systems seem to offer some useful organisational tools for the knowledge engineer. At their present level of development these systems are little more than intelligent word-processors with a powerful user interface and graphical capabilities. When a tool is useful it should be used; however, there are no recommendations in this book as to what packages the knowledge engineer should use. The remit here is limited to describing the knowledge elicitation situation and various techniques. In the near future there may well be powerful automatic elicitation systems. Until then, it appears that knowledge engineers will have to do most of the work themselves.

The rest of this book is organised in the following way:

Chapter 2: This is a highly speculative analysis of expertise, resulting in a basic principle which underpins the knowledge acquisition methodology outlined in this book. The purpose of this chapter is to stimulate if not enlighten the reader. There are many ways to explore the concept of expertise or knowledge; readers may like to develop their own analysis after reading this chapter.

Chapter 3: This is a comparison between knowledge elicitation and other forms of social interaction focussing upon the roles of the systems analyst and knowledge engineer.

Chapter 4: The subject matter for this chapter is interviewing theory relevant to knowledge elicitation. This is a subset of interviewing theory as a whole and therefore is a short but important chapter. The chapter concludes with an overview of the issues which concern the user of the expert system.

Chapter 5: This chapter describes in detail the major knowledge elicitation techniques.

Chapter 6: The first meeting and first interview between the knowledge engineer and the expert is very important. This chapter presents the content of the first meeting and a selection of questions which should be asked of the expert. Each question is discussed in terms of the reasoning underlying it and the ramifications for feasibility, design and management.

Chapter 7: This chapter deals with the planning and preparation issues involved in holding successful interviews, as well as the preparation and planning which is required for the project as a whole.

Chapter 8: The analysis of the knowledge elicitation interview and of the derived and verified information is the subject of this chapter. A number of intermediate representations are presented and discussed.

Chapter 9: The knowledge engineer writes the feasibility study using the information from the interviews outlined in chapter 6. This chapter describes the main issues which must be covered in that document.

Chapter 10: A recommended project management regime for expert systems is presented in this chapter. The reader is reminded that this area could quite easily form a book on its own. The orientation here is project management with emphasis on the knowledge acquisition.

Chapter 11: In order to pull together the ideas from the previous ten chapters a case study is presented. The case study in question is the ALVEY EMEX project.

# 2

# The nature of expertise and knowledge acquisition

## INTRODUCTION

The proposition that comprehending the nature of knowledge facilitates the building of expert systems is mistaken. Knowledge is a difficult concept to define. The constituents of knowledge, such as inference, experience, memory and certainty, require a complex conceptual analysis in their own right before the analysis of knowledge can proceed. The concept of expertise is more appropriate as it is more narrowly defined. This chapter describes a suggested framework for knowledge acquisition based upon an analysis of expertise. The veracity or utility of the principles underlying the framework are not important in their own right. Unlike the rest of this book the intention in this chapter is to explore some of the deeper issues. This is the only chapter which is oriented towards a more philosophical perspective. This chapter is here to be provocative and to be criticised. Its function is to make the reader think. The suggested knowledge acquisition framework is an incidental but nevertheless valuable result of the analysis. There is no requirement for knowledge engineers to consider at length what expertise is or any other related issues. However, knowledge engineers are by inclination curious and inquisitive people!

Expertise is directly related to what is done: it can be categorised in terms of an occupational category, such as lawer (legal), surgeon (medical) or social worker (caring services). Expertise has a psychological basis: it stems from memory, perception and problem solving skills and exists only in a social context which is, after all, where the expert system must reside. The analysis of expertise proceeds by asking, can an expert system be built to encapsulate any form of expertise? Are there some forms of expertise which would not be considered suitable for expert systems? This is really an enquiry into practicalities as well as the beginning of a philosophical discussion. The first step is to discover the mental and behavioural bases of expertise and then associate these with particular occupations.

## FACTORING EXPERTISE

The analysis of expertise begins by identifying six factors, combinations of which may be used to describe any type of expertise which underlies a particular occupation. This does not imply that this is the only way of categorising expertise. The six factors are cognitive processing, judgemental behaviour, social behaviour backed by social knowledge, creative behaviour, analytic behaviour, and the following of strict procedures or scripts. Before the factors are combined here are some brief definitions of each factor.

Cognitive processing refers to the tasks which can be performed by a person without the need for conscious thought. There must have been a period of learning and an associated period of assimilation before the individual could perform the task without thinking about it. Riding a bicycle, copy typing or controlling a motorcar are examples. Judgemental refers to the mental capacity to make decisions, weigh up evidence and assess the consequences.

Social knowledge is the basis of all our common sense with respect to the social world rather than the physical world. Social knowledge is so all-encompassing that a precise definition is difficult to construct. It consists of experiences of social contact from our early years and includes expectations of behaviour and mores of conduct.

Creativity is that mysterious element which has baffled psychologists since the beginning of that science. Creativity has to do with insight, inspiration, the left-hand side of the brain, madness and who knows what else.

Analysis is a particular type of thinking which transforms one representation into one or more different representations making it easier to perceive particular meanings which were not evident in a previous representation. A simple example is an array of test scores for a class of children over many different subjects which explains how well each child did in each subject but does not provide any comparison between subjects. By transforming the raw scores for each test into a 'z' score by a statistical analysis. The result is a measure which can be used to make comparisons across subjects but is removed from the reality of how many questioned questions were answered correctly and how many were not.

Finally, procedural behaviour refers to the repetitive following of a script or procedure such as a list of instructions. Most factory work utilises this factor. When people become practised at following the same routine they become more efficient (or at least so theory informs us). Expertise may be described as a combination of these factors but the factors themselves are not independent and tend to overlap. The next stage of the analysis looks at four groups of these overlapping combinations. The reader may wish to consider overlaps which are not dealt with here.

Cognition and judgemental behaviour have a tendency to overlap as shown by those judgements which are made with very little conscious thought. Take, for example, the sort of judgements made by an experienced driver in traffic. In a narrow street with some parked cars a driver may find herself either virtually stopped or quickly darting through a gap before she realises that the oncoming traffic is a problem. The second combination is that of judgemental and social knowledge. Social knowledge is a static store of facts dealing with most aspects of our everyday life. The combination with judgemental behaviour makes the social knowledge dynamic. It means we can act as social beings. The third combination concerns the overlap between creativity and analytical behaviour. This is demonstrated when invention and analysis coalesce to result in a particular representational transformation or problem solving technique which may be described as an elegant solution. The final combination of analysis and procedural behaviour is concerned with the routine breakdown of information — leading to anything but an elegant solution.

The next stage is to divide the factors into two groups of three on the basis of the overlaps. The first of these groupings, labelled the mental states continuum, is presented in Fig. 2.1.

| Deep cognitive skills | / / | Judgemental skills | / / | High-level social skills |

Fig. 2.1 — The mental states continuum.

The mental states continuum represents from left to right the change from the amoral, non-conscious domain of pure cognition to the moral, meaningful and significant representation of the social world.

The second grouping of factors is the behavioural continuum. This deals with what people do and the modes in which people interact with the world. This continuum moves from the mysterious creative to the anything but mysterious procedural.

| Highly creative | / / | Analytical | / / | Strict procedural |

Fig. 2.2 — The behavioural components of expertise.

Each type of expertise can be related to a particular occupation. The mental states continuum and associated occupations is presented in Fig. 2.3.

| Deep congintive skills | Judgemental skills | High-level social skills |
| --- | --- | --- |
| typist, juggler | senior manager | social worker |

Fig. 2.3 — Mental components of expertise.

When expertise is low in social content it is usually manifested in a deeply cognitive form. The skills possessed by a fast and accurate typist or a juggler are examples of this deeply cognitive expertise. This form of expertise is internalised through practice. It must be made clear here that it is only the core of the expertise which is being discussed. Typists do more than hit keys with fingers but the physical operations needed to type at an acceptable speed are performed without conscious thought. Virtually all expert physical activities, such as sporting prowess, fall into this category. There is also an experiential and creative component which separates the great from the good.

Judgemental expertise is certainly the domain of the professional problem solver. Highly skilled management fall into this category. Any occupation which has as a major component decision making is included if the decision making is characterised by flexibility. Expertise which uses social knowledge often involves working directly with people in the role of helper rather than co-worker. For example, the social worker who is in immediate contact with her clients requires a working knowledge of people, both formal and informal theories of people and the laws which relate to people. The journalist or author (of fiction) are obvious candidates for this category too, as is the social scientist. Authors of fiction may have little contact with people when writing books but they require a great amount of social knowledge in order to perform their task. Of course they need a working knowledge of the English language and a particular style of writing too. The author's social knowledge does not have to be greater than that of someone who has never thought of writing a book. What is suggested is that the expertise or knowledge needed to write a novel relies on our social memory and that this memory is put to work. High level social skills require vast amounts of social knowledge. Social knowledge is concerned with people, and everything done by people when acting in groups. It is interesting to speculate on the boundaries of social knowledge and its representations.

The behavioural components of expertise are described in Fig. 2.4.

| Highly creative | Judgemental | Strict procedural |
|---|---|---|
| musician | programmer, driver | typist |

Fig. 2.4 — The behavioural components of expertise.

The first behavioural factor is creativity. The form of the product of a creative skill cannot be predicted in advance. The creative solution is generally unique, at least to the person involved, although there may be similarities with previous solutions to similar problems. While the form of the final product is ultimately constrained, the exact method by which it is achieved is not known in advance.

The second behavioural factor is analysis. The mathematician and the scientist are examples of occupations which are based on this form of expertise.

The third behavioural factor is procedural. This is the rule of the conveyor belt. A vast amount of factory work has as its basis repetitive actions. This differs from the behaviour exhibited in the deep cognitive classification in that the parts of the whole process may be quite complex requiring particular spatial skills. The worker has to stay conscious but there is little scope for invention or deviation from the regime.

This has been leading to the final representation of expertise and occupations in order that the original enquiry may be answered. That inquiry was, can an expert system be built to encapsulate any type of expertise? In this final representation the two continua have been combined to produce Fig. 2.5, a 3×3 table representing the structure of expertise in

|  | Deep cognitive skills | Judgemental skills | High-level social skills |
|---|---|---|---|
| Highly creative | Musician | Senior management | Author, poet |
| Analytical | Mathematician | Economist, programmer | Social scientist |
| Strict procedural | Typist | Driver | Social worker |

Fig. 2.5 — The mental and behavioural components of expertise.

terms of its mental and behavioural components.

Using Fig. 2.5 will assist with the answer to the basic enquiry, which types of expertise are applicable to expert systems technology?

Of all the occupational categories described, the placement of the social worker in relation to the others causes the greatest disagreement. The reader is invited to think of a replacement, an occupation which combines a high degree of social knowledge and possibly social skills and which in essence is very procedural. The reason the social worker came to mind is because social workers tend to follow policy conventions within a strict legal framework. The author apoligises to all social workers, friends of social workers and any other occupational group which feels badly done by in this analysis. It is the underlying structure of the expertise that is of interest, not the subjective interpretations of the occupational role.

Those types of expertise which demonstrate an inherent difficulty to expert system development will be rejected, beginning with the applicability of social knowledge. Social knowledge is about people. It is more important to use than any other type of knowledge. Social knowledge may not be used at work, but without it we would be unable to work. The fundamental fact about social knowledge is that there is a lot of it. Social knowledge covers a vast amount of different topics at such a high level of abstraction that there appears to be no other place for storing it but the human head. Accordingly, the fundamental problem with social knowledge is the problem of storage (and representation). Therefore, in one stroke the boxes which fall under the mental category of social knowledge can be dispensed with.

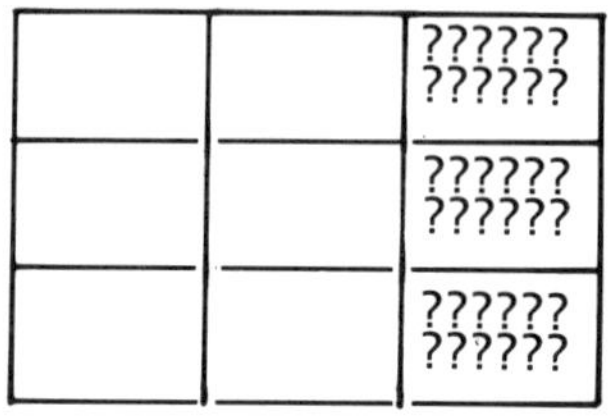

Fig. 2.6 — Too much social knowledge to store.

The reason for excluding a factor from those which are amenable to expert systems technology is not only that the underlying characteristics of the expertise cannot form the basis of a knowledge-base but also for commercial reasons. A bookkeeping knowledge-base is perfectly feasible from a technical point of view but makes no commercial sense as the cost of knowledge analysis is proscriptive for an application which is suited to conventional data processing. Those occupations are associated with the strictly procedural factor and therefore not applicable to expert systems.

Fig. 2.7 — Procedural expertise does not require expert systems technology.

Those types of expertise based upon deeply cognitive knowledge require a coherent and specific theory of cognition. No theory of cognition is specific enough to be considered as the basis of a knowledge-base thus cognitive forms of expertise are not yet amenable to knowledge-based systems. Further research in cognitive modelling may mean that human cognitive processes can be simulated by a computer system. At this point then, cognition and expert systems will find some form of accommodation. However, it remains to be seen if this will be more efficient than mechanistic or behavioural replications.

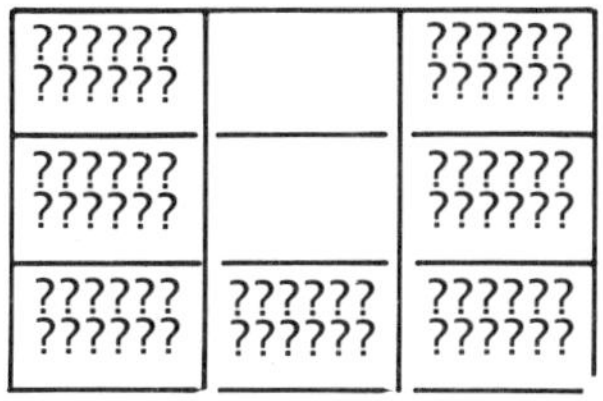

Fig. 2.8 — No coherent and specific theory of cognition.

The objection to cognitive forms of expertise is very similar to the objection to expertise with a significant creative component. At the present time there is no operational theory of creativity or even a clear understanding of what creativity means. Some optimism may be found in the fact that workers in artificial intelligence find learning and creativity one of the most interesting and important areas for research. However, it would seem that it will not be until a much later date that expertise with a high degree of creativity will be within the grasp of knowledge-based systems.

Fig. 2.9 — Creativity is too complex at this time.

The last form of expertise which consists of a mixture of the analytical and judgemental is applicable to current expert systems technology. Expertise requiring analysis grounded within a strictly defined domain offers the best opportunity for implementation if the amount of deep cognitive skills and common sense knowledge can be limited and controlled. Expertise in which judgements are made in the full knowledge of the current situation and with guidance from experience or theory also provides an exploitable basis for the construction of a knowledge-base. It is where judgements are made creatively or without a real understanding of the underlying circumstances that problems will occur — this is the basis of what knowledge engineers call uncertainty. It is difficult to build a knowledge-base based on intuition.

Without doubt, every occupation has, to a degree, elements from types of expertise other than what has been described here as the core type. The typist must use her knowledge of what is or is not applicable in such a document without this being made explicit. And she may use creative solutions to particular problems, especially if she is using a good word-processor. The expertise identified as applicable to current expert systems technology will include creativity, strictly defined procedural behaviour, unconscious cognitive processing as well as some commonsense (social) knowledge combined to make that particular 'expert brew'. The problems in dealing with unspecified forms of expertise will be present in all domains. The procedure of disentangling the understandable analytical and judgemental processes from other sources of knowledge allows the knowledge engineer to isolate and control the less tractable forms of knowledge.

A basis for a knowledge acquisition methodology can be formulated following the analysis of expertise presented above. Firstly, ascertain the domain characteristics of the expertise with reference to the behavioural and mental dimensions. This can be derived from and in tandem with a categorisation or typology of the domain objects. This concentration upon domain characteristics, as opposed to the task, has a number of other benefits which will be dealt with in later chapters. Secondly, isolate and investigate the analytical methods used by the expert. Thirdly, pay attention to the judgemental behaviour of the expert with respect to the situation in which this behaviour occurs and the heuristics which guide it. Fourthly, categorise the residue into its degree of creative or commonsense (etc.) components. Invent fixes to include the non-specific expertise in the system, or ways it could be excluded (by involving the user, for example).

If the above is the bare bones of a knowledge elicitation methodology, what does the flesh consist of? First and foremost, knowledge acquisition is concerned with interviewing. This leads inevitably to the collection of a number of transcripts. These transcripts must be analysed. Knowledge engineers have developed specific forms of analysis techniques. The utility of these techniques has rarely been verified by anyone other than their proponents, so the readers are on their own in this area. A number of these techniques are demonstrated, but not always evaluated, in chapter 8.

Lastly, the third component to knowledge engineering is implementation. This must take place in some programming or knowledge engineering environment. To some extent the principles and practices of implementation are determined by the software environment, the domain and requirements of the users. There are a number of developing ideas which are intended to be all-encompassing and these can be found in the recent literature on expert systems. No attempt has been made in this book to delve deeply into the area of implementation.

The three strands of knowledge engineering — knowledge elicitation, knowledge analysis and implementation — are bound together by a project management strategy which is the subject of chapter 10. The author feels that much more can be and should be said on the subject of the management of expert systems projects than appears in this book but is unable to recommend any recent texts which provide this information.

**SUMMARY**
- Expertise is an easier concept to understand than knowledge
- The major factors which describe expertise are cognitive processing, judgemental behaviour, social behaviour, creativity, analysis, and strictly procedural.
- The basis of the knowledge acquisition methodology is:
  — ascertain the domain characteristics of the expertise
  — investigate the analytical methods used by the expert
  — investigate the judgemental behaviour which the expert displays
  — categorise the residue of the expertise and decide how to implement this.

# 3

# Knowledge elicitation as a social situation

**INTRODUCTION**

Knowledge elicitation is a unique social process. In order to understand it, we must make comparisons with other similar social processes such as an ordinary conversation, a psychological experiment, opinion polling, a police interrogation and systems analysis. Because of particularly close similarities there will be a more detailed comparison with systems analysis at the end of this chapter.

Attributes in common to all these situations are: the purpose of the interaction, the motives of the participants, the location and its importance, the roles and status of the participants, the length of the interview and degree of reoccurrence, the type of information sought and the specificity of that information.

The most common of all forms of social intercourse is the **conversation**. Conversations take place at work, at home, in the street or the public bar, virtually anywhere in fact. The purpose of a conversation is social and the motives of the interlocutors is assumed to be the same — that of sustaining their social identity and the society they live in. You may only talk to people once in your lifetime or may talk to them every day for many years. The subject matter may be recollections, facts or opinions. Generally, specific details or exactitude is not required. There are times when knowledge elicitation seems like an ordinary conversation. This implies that the expert and knowledge engineer have succeeded in developing a good working relationship and the knowledge engineer is acquainted with the domain. The only incongruous factor is the specificity of the information.

The **psychological interview** as the method of performing a psychology experiment exists to increase the stock of psychological knowledge by testing a specific hypothesis. This is, presumably, the motive of the experimenter but not necessarily the motive of the subject who may feel under a social or academic obligation to participate. Participation may be rewarded financially, but this is unlikely. Psychological experiments usually take place in a laboratory. If they do not, which is rare, the ethos of the laboratory is carried by the experimenter to the location. This is a result of the status of the experimenter as a psychologist and the social status (or stigma) given to psychology. The status of subject is comparatively low. The roles of subject and experimenter are rigidly defined and strictly adhered to. It is usual for psychological experiments to have a short duration and non-serial nature. The information derived is quite specific and deals either directly, or indirectly, with the mental states of the subjects. The attitudes and feelings of the expert are not the central concern of the knowledge engineer, unless they are likely to hinder the efficient transmission of information. A final difference between the knowledge elicitation and the psychology experiment is in the atmosphere, where it is unusual for the structured solemnity of the psychological experiment to pervade the knowledge elicitation sessions.

The **opinion poll** is also similar to a psychological experiment. It differs in having a commercial orientation as its purpose — some one is paying for it. The instrumental motive guides the poller while the polled is motivated by social reasons. The commercial orientation pervades knowledge elicitation to a greater degree. The cost of knowledge engineering is much higher than opinion polling. We must assume that the expert is charged at a prime rate and the 'opinionators' come free of charge.

The **police interrogation** exists to find the truth. The motivation for the police officer is to catch the criminal and for the suspect it is either to avoid being caught or to prove her innocence and assist the police in finding the perpetrators. The suspect knows that even innocent people are caught sometimes. In the police interrogation the status difference is more pronounced than in any other type of interview. Police interrogations may last many times longer than the optimum knowledge elicitation interview. It is unlikely, however, that there will be as many interrogations as knowledge elicitation interviews or that the elapsed time for an interrogation will last longer than the knowledge elicitation required of a large expert system — the difference being between intensity and longevity.

The information required by the police is concerned with actions and reasons, with a high degree of specificity and validity. Occasionally the knowledge engineer has to interrogate the expert in a manner similar to that of a police interrogation. The differences are in the status, roles, raison d'être, and elapsed time. The differences far outweigh the similarities.

**Systems analysis** is very similar to knowledge elicitation. It differs, by concentrating upon more procedural information. System analysis interviews are not likely to be prolonged over more than three sessions. The analyst may also profess to a greater status than the person providing the information. Before commencing a more detailed comparison between systems analysis and knowledge elicitation, the description of knowledge elicitation will be given in line with the previous descriptions.

Knowledge elicitation, like systems analysis and opinion polling, has a commercial orientation. Although research has been predominant in the past, it would appear such days are now over. The motivation of the participants is to provide a form of expertise suitable for implementation. If the expert does not share this common goal then problems may arise. The location is of some importance: it should be suitable for detailed inquiry. The roles of the participants are obviously different, however, there should be little or no status differences. The major distinguishing factor is elapsed time. This may be well over a year — with perhaps fifty or more interviews of about two hours duration. The information required concerns procedures, reasons, theories, decisions and the specific meanings of concepts.

The closeness of systems analysis to knowledge elicitation requires a more detailed examination. The similarity between the two occupations suggests that the acquisition of the skills needed by a knowledge engineer would be comparatively simple for the trained systems analyst. Many tasks are common to both groups. However, not all the tasks of a systems analyst will be performed by the knowledge engineer (and vice versa) and differences in detail exist within the same tasks.

The typical systems analyst, if there is such a person, is involved in project selection, the feasibility study, analysis, design and the development and testing of the system, as well as changeover and use.

The knowledge engineer with specific responsibility for knowledge acquisition should be involved with the project selection, feasibility study, project planning, knowledge elicitation, software design, writing the knowledge-base, validation of the knowledge and maintaining the knowledge-base.

To what extent the knowledge engineer is actually involved in all of these tasks is debatable. This discussion is made more problematic by the lack of a recognised occupational definition of a knowledge engineer. It will be necessary to take a personal view on what constitutes the ideal type of knowledge engineer. This statement is based upon personal experience and appreciation of other authors' opinions.

Both the systems analyst and the knowledge engineer are involved in the selection of the project. Expert systems projects have historically owed more to the result of political (with a small 'p') than commercial decisions. In these circumstances the knowledge engineer's input has carried little weight. Currently, expert systems are becoming recognised as offering a commercial advantage to the users of such systems. Commercial realities, specifically the large financial risk to client and contractor, will revalue the knowledge engineer's input.

The feasibility study is an area where the knowledge engineer provides an important function. The feasibility study does not only result in a document which pronounces upon the feasibility of the project. The project is obviously feasible, otherwise no one would go to the expense of commissioning a feasibility study (which everyone knows is going to say the project is feasible). The utility of this document is as an input to the planning stage of the project. Another important corollary is the contact made between the knowledge engineer and the domain experts.

Systems analysis tends to place greater emphasis on the costs and benefits of the proposed system as the commercial feasibility of the system is under investigation. Problems in detailing the costs involved in an expert systems project and the possible shortfall on the benefits have limited the effectiveness of the cost/benefit analysis in the feasibility study. There is a large problem with estimating the costs of the system development, in particular the knowledge elicitation phase. If the costs of building a system cannot be adequately estimated then a cost/benefit analysis is difficult to perform. Investing in expert system technology is not for the faint-hearted. Both the systems analyst and knowledge engineer are concerned with the major requirements and necessary features of the system. However, expert system projects have not placed a great deal of emphasis on a detailed specification at the outset but have developed a cyclical development which feeds off the knowledge analysis.

Analysis is to system design what knowledge elicitation is to knowledge engineering. This is where the greatest differences lie. Analysis is the detailed study and evaluation of the current system. The result is a model of the new system in terms of data storage, data-flows, inputs and outputs. Knowledge elicitation is the systematic study of the domain of expertise; the result is a record of that study in terms of a number of knowledge engineering documents and intermediate representations. Through analysis, that record is transferred into a functioning knowledge-base. The system analyst follows the analysis phase with a design of the new system. This is the transformation of the logical model of the system into a number of detailed specifications of the parts of the system.

The knowledge engineer (knowledge elicitor) is less likely to have a large input at the system design stage. This is contingent upon personal experience. It is possible that a knowledge engineer with system design background is responsible for knowledge elicitation. This seems a waste of human resources, unless the contracting organisation has a surplus of software engineers. As a managerial point it is advisable to have a software engineer conversant with expert system software design involved in this task. Rather than a specific design, the elicitor sketches the broad outline of the system using the structure of domain knowledge gleaned from the orientation/feasibility study. The knowledge engineer also provides tentative specifications for the user interface, using the input from the interviews with the potential users. The detailed software design should be left to the software engineering experts.

In the development and testing phase of conventional software the analyst is on hand to supervise the writing of code. Design changes are made only when the current design becomes untenable. There is a greater emphasis in conventional systems on getting it right first time. In comparison the development of an expert system has historically relied upon design flexibility with a process known as rapid prototyping. Expert systems development is cyclic with the emphasis on getting progressively closer to the expert's refined method on the basis that this method is too complex to achieve in one go but requires many iterations of the refine, extend and debug cycle.

In knowledge engineering the pace tends to be less variable. During the main phase of an expert system project elicitation proceeds as in the orientation phase. A basic knowledge-base is built and through iteration this is validated and extended. The basic design is evaluated with respect to the first running knowledge-base and is then refined, changed and rewritten. The documentation, help and explanation features originate from the knowledge elicitation sessions and are edited into usable forms as a byproduct of gaining a deeper insight into the domain.

Perhaps the most hectic time for the systems analyst comes when the system first comes on stream. In comparison the knowledge engineer's work is tailing off. A knowledge-base has either been proved during its incremental development or has failed to come close to the expectations. There is little that hectic activity can achieve. Paradoxically, a very successful implementation using expert systems technology may produce a greater work load as the clients invest in adventurous extensions to the proven technology.

Knowledge acquisition has three major subdivisions: interviewing, analysis and implementation. Knowledge engineering, of which knowledge acquisition is but a sub-division, is concerned with three people. The least important person is the knowledge engineer, he is there to do the work. The second most important person is the expert; if she is not available or is incapable of communicating the expertise then there is no expert system. The most important person is the actual user of the system. Initially this will be a hypothetical person; even so, he must be identified and his needs and capabilities must be understood. An expert system is only an expert system if it is used by someone. This depends upon the knowledge engineer designing the system to be used by the person he has identified as the user. This chapter is completed by a report of a paper by Collins, Green and Draper (1985) which sets out the basic philosophy concerning the nature of the user with respect to an expert system.

Collins, Green and Draper begin their analysis by describing expert systems as a medium for the transmission of knowledge between an expert and a naive end-user, a transmission which is more efficient than most other media of knowledge transfer, face-to-face communication being a notable exception. Central to their ideas is the concept of tacit knowledge. They use this concept to explain the developmental potential of expert systems.

The most endearing aspect of the Collins *et al.* paper is the metaphor used to describe the expertise which the expert pours into the system and which the user takes out of it. This they describe as being like chicken soup with dumplings and the expert system is like the colander which allows the soup to escape but captures the dumplings. The soup is the tacit knowledge — the context or meaning of facts, the taken-for-granted assumptions which are generally not articulated. The dumplings are the readily explicable facets of knowledge such as facts and heuristics.

Most work in improving expert systems, this book included, is directed at making the holes in the colander as small as possible. The current situation, with gigantic holes in the colanders, depends upon users supplying their own soup to complete the meal.

The problem with expert systems is the loss of this tacit knowledge either because it escapes elicitation or escapes representation. The possible solution of reducing the size of the holes is admirable but impracticable. A more positive solution is to use the tacit knowledge held by the users as an indication of the scope of the system. This requires a coherent analysis of the users' state of knowledge with respect to the expertise — how much soup they have. Only when the knowledge engineer has a clear idea of the status of the users' tacit knowledge can he elicit the knowledge with respect to those users.

You are left with these thoughts while we now try to reduce the size of the holes in that colander.

## SUMMARY

- Comparisons with other social situations help to understand knowledge elicitation
- Significant attributes used to compare social situations are:
  - the purpose of the interaction
  - the motives of the participants
  - the location and its importance
  - roles and status of participants
  - length and degree of reoccurrence of the interview
  - type and specificity of the information sought
- Estimating the cost of knowledge elicitation is a big problem
- Unlike conventional data processing, projects knowledge engineering has not placed a great deal of emphasis on a detailed specification but uses a cyclical development which requires the knowledge analysis approach as one of the major inputs
- The cyclical development allows the knowledge engineer to refine and extend the knowledge-base so as to achieve the closest approximation to the expert's method
- One way to envisage knowledge elicitation is as chicken soup and dumplings being poured through a sieve
- The greatest difference between conventional data processing projects and knowledge-based systems is the difference between systems analysis and knowledge elicitation

# 4

# Interviewing theory

**INTRODUCTION**

Knowledge acquisition consists of interviewing, analysis and implementation. This chapter is concerned with the theory of interviewing. Interviewing techniques and other knowledge acquisition techniques will be presented in the next chapter. The major issues covered in this chapter are concerned with the participants to the interview, their reason for, and problems with, participation, the nature of the question and the answer, how transitions from one topic to another take place and what factors dictate the pace of the interview. There are two major participants to the interview: the asker and the asked. From the perspective of knowledge elicitation these will be referred to as the knowledge engineer (he) and the expert (she) respectively. The final section in this chapter concerns the potential user of the system. The topic of who the user is returns throughout the book, and the end of this chapter acts as an introduction.

The expert will generally be well educated and well qualified, have high status in her organisation, and may well have a managerial role. Exceptions include a valued and skilled shop floor operative or a highly experienced 'sole trader' such as a Scottish hill farmer. Exceptions aside, her occupational situation suggests that she will be more used to asking questions and receiving answers than vice versa.

The background, experience and status of the knowledge engineer is less clear cut. It is very likely that he will have been educated up to degree level and a strong possibility that he has a background in computer science and data processing. Some knowledge engineers have an academic qualification in artificial intelligence, psychology or the social sciences. Whatever the particular career of the knowledge engineer has been, he must project an image of professionalism and competence. This is taken on trust in the initial meetings but will be tested as the project progresses. Any evidence of incompetence shown by the knowledge engineer may reduce the active participation of the expert. Incompetence may be manifested as a lack of organisation, bad time-keeping or a display of limited understanding when a fuller comprehension had been expected.

The competence and more importantly the image of competence is one of the factors which determine the degree of participation during knowledge elicitation phase. Long-term and consistent commitment is necessary from both of the major participants for the success of the project. In the case of the knowledge engineer it is assumed that he is committed to the success of the project. If this is not the case it is very likely the project will fail. If the expert realises the knowledge engineer has a low degree of participation this will inevitably reduce her own.

The expert's degree of participation is dependent upon more than her perception of the knowledge engineer's commitment to the project. Depending upon the expert's status within her organisation she may well be following orders to participate. This does not guarantee full participation over time as she may see the project as being a threat to her livelihood or a hindrance to her main occupation and therefore a major imposition. It is, therefore, worth asking the expert what her reasons are for participating and her feelings regarding the project.

Altruism is one reason for expert participation in the project. Commercial considerations aside, the system may be of benefit to the world, poor nations or the less well-off. Although benefit to humanity as a whole and financial gain are not mutually exclusive they seldom overlap. However, if the expert's altruism can be utilised irrespective of the commercial imperatives which govern the direction of the project the knowledge engineer will have an eager and helpful expert as a co-worker.

The expert may exhibit a personality which is oriented to helping the knowledge engineer. This is altruism on a smaller scale, but it is still a benefit to the knowledge engineer. Only in exceptional cases will some sort of display of altruism not be the case. In those cases where the expert has a hostile or uncooperative nature the elicitation of knowledge is going to be very difficult and the success of the project is in jeopardy. Although this is a very obvious point it is surprising to note that some knowledge engineers are expected to elicit knowledge from experts who have no interest in the success of the project and possibly a desire to see the project terminated. Sometimes the expert's belligerence and hostility can be very subtle and restrained, but this is no substitute for active participation. An experienced knowledge engineer will soon realise that his expert is not committed to the project and attempt to find a solution to the potential problems that this raises. Solutions range from finding some other source of knowledge which includes another expert or finding a way by which the current expert can participate more fully than previously.

The ego of the expert, and the boost it receives from being put on a pedestal and asked a lot of questions, is an important contributing factor to the overall enthusiasm of the expert for the project. Other forms of intellectual satisfaction can be achieved by developing a more active role in the development of the system. The knowledge elicitation sessions and the later implementation considerations become a new challenge. Knowledge engineering can be a particularly interesting enterprise to the expert who has achieved all the accolades possible in her own domain. If the expert likes an intellectual challenge she will like the challenge of producing a successful expert system.

Material benefits may assure the expert's participation: either the use of the expert system and a share of the rights or a high consultancy rate are obvious incentives. However, the incentive of greater financial benefits may pale as time passes.

Feedback may be used to increase the expert's enthusiasm for the project. Discussion between the expert and knowledge engineer on the content and form of the interviews involves the expert without greatly increasing the workload. In fact, acting upon the expert's suggestions may reduce the overall work load.

Participation is reduced by the demands of the particular situation. The first demand is the time the expert must set aside, time which will probably be very precious to her. In total this is likely to be a lot of time. Coupled with this are the difficulties and repetition involved in knowledge elicitation which are obvious disincentives to participation. The idea of holding thirty or more interviews with the expert over the next year may be fine from the point of the knowledge engineer but the expert may not be inclined to think the same. The scale of the knowledge elicitation should be made clear to the expert at an early date so alternative arrangements, such as using a less experienced expert for particular topics, can be made.

The unfamiliarity of the structure of the knowledge elicitation sessions may be quite stressful, particularly if the expert is not used to social situations. This last point may escape most readers. Knowledge engineers should, by their very nature, be skilled in social situations. Some people are not so socially inclined and have no problems in excelling in their chosen field. Others, more socially orientated, are unsure of what is expected from them and this leads to stress and to an unwillingness to participate in the project. It is suggested that a presentation of the knowledge engineering issues is given at an early stage. This demystification of the black art of knowledge engineering is a useful device for reducing the fears of the expert.

The term 'participation' refers to the degree of involvement in the project as a whole, while 'motivation' refers to the degree of involvement in the particular interview. There are many symptoms of the loss of motivation. One such symptom, underreporting, includes yes/no answers when longer replies were expected. The most extreme form of underreporting is silence. Other forms of limited communication may arise because the expert is more interested in personal needs than the interview, such as refreshment or personal telephone calls. Similarly the expert may be easily distracted or even seek distractions. Consistently changing the subject is another indication of the expert's loss of motivation. The value of a knowledge elicitation session with an unmotivated expert is very dubious; the value of exploring the cause of the low motivation is not.

As with participation the social norm is to cooperate. Many of the incentives to participate apply in respect to motivation. One determinate of the expert's motivation is the perceived success of the current and previous interviews. If the expert has no evidence that she is being understood then her desire to continue is reduced. The last point suggests that by providing evidence of progress the degree of motivation throughout the interview can be maintained. Experts identify progress by noting the increased understanding exhibited by the knowledge engineer. Asking more intelligent, or less stupid, questions indicates that this progress is being maintained. Feedback, both in terms of teachback and review (what has been learnt so far) and overviews of the project as a whole or of the interview, may act to increase the expert's degree of motivation. The teachback technique is one in which the knowledge engineer attempts to explain some of the concepts to the expert. The review is the technique in which topics from previous interviews are presented as propositions to the expert for confirmation. Both these techniques are described more fully in the next chapter.

The objective of any interview is to obtain information. However, other objectives may coexist with the main objective. The knowledge engineer may be oriented towards affiliation with the expert — in which working with this famous person has become a major objective in itself. Other secondary objectives would be the desire to exercise control, the desire to show off one's own programming or analysis skills or the definition of a common goal to enhance a sense of achievement. Secondary objectives have a major impact upon the degree of motivation exhibited by the expert. The secondary objectives of the participants and the personalities of the participants are intertwined. The possibility of a personality clash (the irrational conflict between two people) is always there. We soon become aware of other people's personalities and as the knowledge engineer is socially skilled he can develop strategies which enable the course of the interview to progress smoothly. By encouraging feedback, the knowledge engineer can gain valuable information about his own shortcomings as perceived by the expert. Acting upon the expert's criticism can only be beneficial to the project as a whole.

The more information the knowledge engineer attempts to extract from the expert the greater the likelihood that the expert's motivation will be reduced. There appears to be a trade-off between the quantity and quality of information and the expert's current degree of motivation. Techniques to redress the balance are suggested in the next chapter.

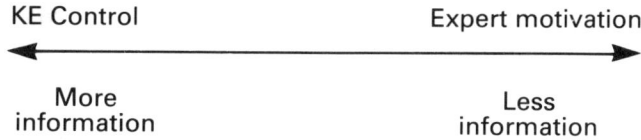

Fig. 4.1.

As motivation is not constant throughout the interview, action will have to be taken to increase the motivation of either the expert or the knowledge engineer. The most obvious action is having a break, refreshments and talk about something other than work. Be aware that this may be seen as a waste of precious time.

Every type of expertise is characterized by a specific vocabulary. One of the first tasks of the knowledge engineer is to extract this vocabulary. This is necessary for several reasons. Firstly, it forms part of the domain analysis which is performed to give the knowledge engineer a basic understanding of the domain. Secondly, using the expert's language allows the knowledge engineer to discuss more complex areas with greater ease than if the expert has to repeatedly translate the more complex terms or use a less specific terminology. Many of the early interviews will be largely concerned with the collection of the domain specific vocabulary. There is a social convention that people communicate without questioning terminology. Sometimes, we nod our heads and agree when we have hardly heard a word that has been said. From the point of view of a knowledge engineer, this convention is a major sin. Any term which is not understood, even if it is a word in common usage but seemingly out of context, must be questioned.

Interviews are about asking questions and receiving answers. The type of answer received will often be determined by the type of question asked. The nature of the answer will determine the type of follow-up question or probe if required. Questions differ in the degree to which they direct the respondent to answer in a specific way. A non-directional question allows the respondent to decide how the question should be answered or even decide which question he wants to answer. Answers do not follow questions as the carriage follows the horse. An example would be an interview with a politician or debate between politicians. An open question gives the respondent the freedom as to the length of the reply. The converse, the closed question, limits the reply to a brief answer, often yes or no. A question may, and probably should, include instructions as to the nature of the expected answer. These instructions are as important as the question itself and more thought should be given to the instructions than to the question. The instruction may relate to the answers of previous questions or knowledge already assimilated. By giving the expert an idea of where the gaps are in the knowledge engineer's understanding the answer will be more relevant.

Although the assimilation of the specific vocabulary is an important part of the knowledge acquisition phase, the knowledge engineer should be careful of using jargon in the questions. A definition of jargon would be terminology which is technical without being explanatory. The wording of the questions should be precise. The knowledge engineer should not use terms which are not understood. Terms only vaguely understood should be the subject of an enquiry on the realisation that this is the case.

Generally, questions should be asked to elicit more information, not to confirm one's own beliefs. The knowledge engineer should avoid questions which begin, 'Is it true that...', or any of the variations. The problem with this format is that if the answer is 'yes' then no more information is provided. If the answer is 'no' it shows some erroneous thinking somewhere along the line. Correcting these errors is constructive, but the real problem arises when the expert fudges the answer or unreasonably qualifies so as to conform, to some degree, with the knowledge engineer's expectations. Therefore always ask a direct question which may begin, 'What do you do when...', and if possible add instructions such as, 'Without going into too much detail tell me what do you do when...'.

The interview should begin with some less demanding topics then move on to more complex issues. This is the examination paper style of questioning. Difficulty is a subjective measure and should be assessed from the knowledge engineer's point of view. The least difficult subjects are probably the unfinished business from the previous interview. With good communication between the knowledge engineer and the expert there should be some consensus as to what areas of the domain will be the most difficult to understand or the most difficult to elicit. Beginning with the easy subject matter allows the participants to get 'warmed up'. The first topic should be the structure of the interview, principally the order of the topics on the agenda.

Answers may be short — one word or a phrase — or long — a half-hour explanation with examples. The answer depends upon the question. If the knowledge engineer has phrased the question well with the correct instructions then the answer should be of the expected type. More detailed and relevant answers are elicited by the probes which follow the initial replies. Answers may lack clarity because the knowledge engineer did not have enough background knowledge. The expert may have given an unclear answer because she misunderstood the knowledge engineer's use of technical terms, indicating a greater level of knowledge than actually exists.

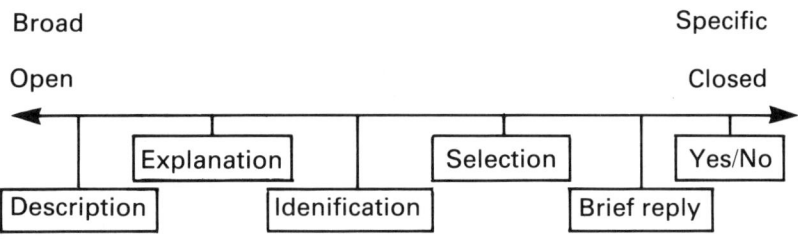

Fig. 4.2 — On questions and answers.

A lack of clarity may arise because the expert finds giving information in this area difficult. She may have problems in expressing herself to someone with little technical background or because information in this area is actually unclear. The knowledge engineer must find the reason for the lack of clarity and develop a strategy to overcome the problem.

An answer may be less specific than the knowledge engineer intended. In this situation the expert must be probed for more information. Restating the question with more adequate instructions may elicit the information to the required degree of specificity. Probes are used to encourage the expert to continue speaking, or to guide her next response in a particular direction. More will be said on the subject of probes in the next chapter.

The utilisation of antecedents is a subtle form of interview control. An antecedent is a subject which was discussed previously. The primary use of an antecedent is to effect an ordered transition from one topic to another. A secondary effect is to increase the expert's degree of motivation or the knowledge engineer's degree of control. Making a transition by referring to a subject which the expert mentioned but which was not taken up by the knowledge engineer in any detail at the time gives the expert a greater sense of involvement. Theory suggests that the older the antecedent the greater the feeling of involvement. The opposite is also true: by not using any of the expert's antecedents the expert feels less involved. The knowledge engineer should keep a list of antecedents which may be used when the expert's involvement seems to be flagging.

The aim of the knowledge elicitation interview is to obtain accurate information. The presence of bias will lead to problems at later stages. Bias may be defined as a systematic distortion without actually being incorrect. The source of bias may be the expert, the knowledge engineer or a breakdown in communication between them. Bias stemming from the expert is unfortunate as it may not be discovered until discrepancies appear in the performance of the running system. The knowledge engineer may, and to some extent must, introduce bias into the system. Any implementation strategy is a form of bias in itself as there is no perfect representation for knowledge inside the computer. The knowledge engineer must become more aware of the processes by which bias can be introduced. One of the most common of all bad practices is the leading question. The most famous of all leading questions is, 'When did you stop beating your wife?' No matter how the respondent answers he is a self-confessed wife-beater. For non-wife-beaters the reply should be, 'I do not beat my wife', which avoids the question. A leading question is a question which implies a situation exists and influences the direction of the response. Knowledge engineers may be guilty of this if they attempt to verify information before obtaining it.

Bias is more often than not the result of unjustified expectations held by the knowledge engineer. This type of bias can enter the system at any time. If unrealistic expectations find their way into the system during analysis and/or implementation then the expert must correct this during review, teachback or by commenting upon the performance of the running system or knowledge-base. The knowledge engineer will probably be totally unaware of the existence of bias which enters the system after the interview. During analysis and implementation the knowledge engineer must make many decisions. He will of course make some bad ones. Therefore, the knowledge must be checked as rigorously as it was obtained. Knowledge acquisition does not come to an end because the knowledge-base has been written.

Bias may enter the system during the elicitation sessions because the knowledge engineer asks leading questions or questions based upon an incorrect premise. The knowledge engineer is advised to reduce his reliance on premises especially early in the project. This is another example of a little knowledge being a dangerous thing. Premises arise from the logical structure of the expertise. If a certain outcome is associated with a particular set of conditions then, when similar conditions are recognised, the knowledge engineer applies what he thinks (perhaps even unconsciously) is the rule and asks a question which has that implied rule as its premise. An analogy is the structure of the English language and the way in which children internalise the rules which underpin this structure before they make allowances for the exceptions. Children are often heard saying 'knowed' instead of 'knew'.

Minor distortions in the knowledge-base can cause problems if they are not corrected, the likelihood being that not all the minor distortions will be corrected. This should not be the case with major distortions. If the knowledge engineer gets something totally wrong then the expert will nearly always put him right. This fact can be used as an aid to validation. If the knowledge engineer is unsure of what is actually the case he can make a statement which he knows is very incorrect in the hope that the minor distortion which motivated the comprehensively incorrect statement will be corrected too. It is better to use this method occasionally than to ask for the information again as the reply may not address the actual confusion.

The knowledge engineer should be aware of who is controlling the pace of the interviews. The pace should be governed by the developing understanding of the knowledge engineer. If the pace of the interview is too fast then the understanding of the knowledge engineer will suffer. This may be rectified at a later stage in the project, when deficiencies are noticed in the knowledge-base. By then there may be too little time to make the required changes. It is more efficient to gain an understanding of the domain from the interviews than from the identification of problems in a poor implementation. If the pace is so slow that too little information is being elicited during the interviews, then once again a poor implementation will result. This time it will not be the understanding of the knowledge engineer which was at fault. Ultimately this will be a problem of project management, although the cause of the less than adequate pace could be from any source.

A symptom of too fast a pace is a high ratio of analysis to interview time coupled with an unacceptably large number of interviews concerned with the same topic. Evidence that the pace is too slow would be a low analysis to interview time ratio and a general dissatisfaction with the results of the analysis of the interview. A rapid pace may well make for short interviews or interviews with a very long agenda. The cause of many of the problems with the interview, including pace, is very likely the result of a poor domain analysis. This topic is covered later.

A rather obvious point, but one which needs making, is that interviews are often improved by better preparation. If a knowledge engineer was totally unprepared for an interview, to the extent of not having prepared an agenda or thought about the general subject area, then success would be dependent upon the expert and luck. The analysis of a previous interview and the preparation for a subsequent one which takes place simultaneously is the subject of chapter 7.

Not all interviews are concerned with audible questions and answers.

The expert or the knowledge engineer may be asked to perform a task or solve a problem. Wherever possible try to utilise a graphical representation. Domains are characterised by formalisms which are used to express ideas. The knowledge engineer must learn this at the same time he is learning the vocabulary.

Always record an interview: audio is usually enough, although sometimes video will be necessary if the expert's task is being demonstrated in a particularly active way. The use of an instant copy camera may be utilised for recording transient examples on marker boards or computer screens. If a computer is being used then a hard copy log of the interaction is essential. The knowledge engineer will have enough to think about in terms of just controlling what is going on and thinking of probes and subject transitions without trying to remember what has been said or attempting to make copious notes. If the expert does not want to be recorded you must explain that progress will be slowed by a factor of ten at least. This is not an empty threat. Also, making notes is a distraction, not only to the knowledge engineer but also to the expert, who will have to restrain herself from having a look to see what is being written about her and what she has said.

The setting of the interview is very important. It should be quiet, free from interruptions and distractions, comfortable with enough room to spread out plans, documents or any other paraphernalia and, most importantly, free from persons who do not have an active role in the process of knowledge elicitation. This most certainly includes management personnel with an insatiable curiosity to find out what this 'knowledge elicitation thing' is all about. These people should be dissuaded from attending the interviews and be presented with recordings or transcripts if they wish to know what the knowledge engineer and expert are getting up to.

## THE USER

The three most important people in an expert systems project are the user, the expert and the knowledge engineer. Their relative importance is in that order. The users, despite being the most important, are often the most neglected. It is obvious why they should not be neglected, but not so obvious why they are, and what can be done to remedy the neglect.

Building an expert system without proper regard to the intended user is like making tea in a pot without a spout. All the effort has been supplied but the fruits of the labour cannot be realised. On balance, a project which takes full account of the user will require a little more effort than one which follows the direction of the implementers and/or the experts, if only because there is a tangible effort in eliciting knowledge and opinions from a potential user group. The effort required to analyse these interviews must also be taken into account.

A disquieting fact for knowledge engineers and any system designers is the likelihood that the optimum way for the user to interact with the software will be different from how the designers and the expert envisaged the system being used. It is important to realise all the restrictions which the user brings to the system before the design process is too far advanced. Even though there is extra effort required in involving the user this may reduce the total effort needed to build the system, owing to the degree of limited interaction which the user can usefully have with the system. Thus, certain interactions and associated functionality with the system, which the expert and the knowledge engineer believed was needed, are revealed to be too complex, too abstruse or beyond the actual scope of the user's interaction with the system.

The first step in the user analysis is the identification of the prospective user. The user analysis is greatly simplified if the intended users are restricted to employees of the company which is supplying the expertise and quite probably the knowledge engineering too. Even greater simplicity is achieved if the user is also an expert. In this case user analysis and expert/domain analysis can be combined.

If the intended user is not an employee of the company which is supplying the expertise then an early objective should be to co-opt a potential user on to the design team. Their attendance is probably only required during the design of the user interface or when modifications to the user interface have been made.

A problem with the expert system application produced for a mass market (not that the author has any knowledge of such a beast) will be the increased cost involved in the user analysis. If the system is intended for use by a number of other companies the designers must generalise as to the roles and current working situations of all the different potential users. However, an expert system which is designed for a mass market transfers any socio-technical/occupational and ergonomic issues to the customers. The introduction of an expert system into one's own company should be proceeded by an analysis of the likely effects of the system upon the intended users and the organisation itself. It must be remembered that the organisation is also a user of the system.

The user analysis should begin early in the life of the project and continue throughout the project until responsibility is transferred to the management of the organisation using the expert system. The user analysis is proceeded by the collection and analysis of information from the expert, known as the domain analysis. The results of the domain analysis are presented in the feasibility study and hopefully this leads to an agreement amongst all the interested parties that a suitable expert system application has been found. Chapter 9, which is concerned with the feasibility study, includes a section dealing with questions for prospective users. Ideally this interview and the analysis of the information should form part of the feasibility study. If it does not, the user analysis should commence as soon as the project goes live.

The user analysis covers three areas, firstly the identification of the user, secondly the mode of use and lastly, predictions concerning the effects of the system on the organisation which intends to use it. The analysis should begin with a critical account of the reasoning behind the selection of the particular application for implementation. However, the knowledge engineer's role is creative as well as constructive. His experience will suggest other uses of and variations to the system over and above the initial conceptualisation. For example a system which advises users on the correct decision to take in particular circumstances may be adapted to be used as a coaching system which explores the consequences of alternative decisions.

Leaving the reasoning behind the choice of application, the knowledge engineer, in concert with others, including the expert, should draw up a list of at least five potential users of the system. The reasoning behind the selection of each group of users is noted, and when the list appears to be complete the priority is to select the target group of users for the first prototype system. The other groups of potential users may be ranked in order of how much their needs differ from the target group, the probable size of the group and estimated degree of intrinsic acceptance. The differing needs of the different users indicate the ease of incorporating another group of users when broadening the system to encompass a greater number of users. The numerical size of a potential user group is indicative of the potential size of the market and a pointer to where the maximum benefit is likely to be. The estimated degree of intrinsic acceptance is a vital factor in determining the commercial success of the system. Some users will have greater difficulty accepting the system than others even though the potential benefit of this group may be higher. With a high degree of resistance the probability of achieving the potential benefits is lower.

Even if the potential users have been identified this process of identifying other groups of users may not be a waste of effort. An alternative approach is to select a user group which it is thought needs a variant of the core system. The importance of this group of potential users may outweigh the original choice causing a review of the original design with particular reference to what effect a change of potential user has upon the feasibility of the original project. If the changes are anything more than trivial a second iteration to the feasibility study may be required before a new design document can be written.

The next step in the user analysis is to understand the role of the potential user in the organisation. This entails a full job description including the user's general function within the company. If this presents more problems than was anticipated then the knowledge engineer must ascertain why. Is it possible that too little thought had gone into defining the potential user group. The objective of user analysis is to gather information so as to be able to fully describe the intended user as he really is. The user analysis should not be used to support a hypothetical profile of the typical user.

The analysis focuses upon the job the target user group currently do, by performing a task analysis on their current tasks including work which has nothing to do with the domain of the expert system, paying particular attention to the times they spend doing certain tasks. A corresponding task analysis concerning the use of the expert system is inferred by the knowledge engineer looking closely at those procedures, if any, the user performs at the present time and which the system will replace. At one extreme the expert system is an aid to user's current task and merely assists with the tasks the user has always performed. At the other extreme the expert system means a complete departure from the user's current tasks. The analysis should detail the differences the expert system will have on the projected user's total work pattern. Finally, the knowledge engineer should assess what the effects will be on the work which has no relation to the domain of expertise. It is possible that the arrival of the expert system may cause problems with the performance of other duties and reduce the predicted overall benefits associated with the introduction of the expert system.

The process of user analysis must include an investigation into the user's model of the proposed system, beginning with what the user knows of the processes and domain of expertise. The user's model of the proposed system includes an account of the processing from the input to output.

The most important role the representative of the user group can play during the development of the system is to assist with the design of the interface, questions and prompts, the level of help and explanation, and with descriptions of the required functionality. This requires attending design meetings in which the useability of the system is explored and constructive criticism of the latest prototype version offered. A representative of the users should attend the project management meetings which take place at the end of each development cycle.

## A CHECKLIST FOR THE USER ANALYSIS

- Who is the user?
  - is the user part of the current company?
  - is the system intended for use by other companies?
  - is this an application for a mass market?
- List five types of potential user:
- if you can't, then why?
- chose one and only one as the target group
- Rank the rest in order of:
  - how much you believe their needs differ from the target group
  - how numerous the group is
  - the estimated degree of intrinsic acceptance
- Detail the target user's current tasks
- Perform a task analysis on the nature of their current tasks, including work which has nothing to do with the expert system
- Take into account the times they spend doing certain tasks
- Infer a task analysis of the user with respect to the expert system
- What procedures do they have to perform at the present time which the system will replace, if any
- What differences will the system have on the projected users total work pattern
- Assess what the effects will be on the work which has no relation to the domain of expertise

## SUMMARY

- The expert will usually be well educated, well qualified, have a high status and probably a managerial role
- Whatever the background of the knowledge engineer he must project an image of professionalism and competence
- Long term and consistent commitment is necessary from both the expert and the knowledge engineer
- Obtain the expert's reasons for participating in the project
- Altruism is one reason for the expert to participate in the project
- Knowledge elicitation will be very difficult if the expert is hostile or has an uncooperative nature
- Appealing to the expert's ego may increase her degree of participation
- Material benefits are a strong incentive to greater expert participation
- Feedback between the expert and knowledge engineer may increase the expert's enthusiasm
- Expert participation is reduced by the demands of the project, such as the time and effort required, the difficulties and repetitive nature of knowledge elicitation
- An overview of knowledge engineering presented to the expert and others is an informative way of beginning the working relationship between the knowledge engineer and the expert
- Whereas participation refers to the degree of involvement in the project over time, motivation refers to the degree of involvement during an interview
- Low motivation may be recognised from symptoms such as underreporting, interest in personal needs, being easily distracted or constantly changing the subject
- One determinate of the expert's motivation is the perceived success of the current and previous interviews
- The major object of knowledge elicitation is to obtain information
- Secondary objects such as an orientation towards affiliation and desire to exercise control also effect the degree of motivation shown by the expert
- There appears to be a trade-off between the quantity or quality of the derived information and the experts degree of participation
- Questions should also include instructions as to the nature of the required answer
- Be very careful about using jargon
- Questions should be asked to elicit more information not confirm one's own beliefs
- The interview should begin with less demanding topics then move on to more complex issues
- A lack of clarity in the expert's answers may indicate she has a problem in explaining herself
- Probes are used to obtain further information after the original question has outlined the topic area
- Antecedents may be used to increase the level of motivation.

- Bias is a systematic distortion of the information
- Do not ask leading questions
- Knowledge acquisition does not come to an end when the knowledge-base has been written
- The pace of the interview should be determined by the knowledge engineer's developing understanding of the expertise
- Interviews are improved by better presentation
- Wherever possible try to utilise a graphical representation
- Always record the interviews
- The setting of the interview is important: it should be quiet, free from distractions and provide ample space to work

# 5

# Techniques for knowledge elicitation

**INTRODUCTION**

The previous chapter was concerned with issues relating directly to interviewing, with a bias towards knowledge elicitation. In this chapter interviewing and other methods of extracting information are described in more detail.

The aim is to provide the reader with the basic skills to follow a strategy in order to achieve a particular goal. The goal of the interview is constrained by the current phase of the project — different elicitation techniques being more appropriate at different phases. In fact the objectives of each phase of the project are achieved by combining a number of different techniques. The structuring of knowledge elicitation techniques which make up a part or whole phase of the project is a managerial issue. However, near the end of this chapter there is a review of a paper by Bainbridge (1986) which deals with the 'horses for courses' issue, of which techniques suit which types of knowledge, while chapter 10 on the management of elicitation presents a suggested structure of techniques within the knowledge elicitation phases of an expert system project.

The combination of effective knowledge elicitation methods with a structured approach is a recipe for a more productive knowledge acquisition phase. The reader is reminded that analysis coupled with preparation is also part of the overall process. The moral of this book is simple: **practice and master the techniques of elicitation and analysis and fit these techniques into the general project management structure**. The efficacy of knowledge acquisition is determined more by those managerial aspects of the project which impinge upon knowledge acquisition than the techniques themselves. However, performance of the techniques is a factor which concerns the knowledge engineer directly and which only they are responsible for.

**OVERVIEW OF THE KNOWLEDGE ELICITATION SESSION**

In the previous chapter there were two roles: the knowledge engineer was the interviewer and the expert the respondent. But things are seldom so simple. In current practice the role of the knowledge engineer is unclear. Some writers on this subject (Hart, 1986) recommend the knowledge engineer should research the subject area before meeting the expert. This acquaintance with the domain is intended to save time. Before the knowledge engineer has walked through the expert's door he already knows some of the vocabulary and some basic text book facts. He is able to converse with the expert from the outset using some of the specialised domain vocabulary.

In my view this is an error. The major reason is that the role of the knowledge engineer is ambivalent from the outset. He talks like an expert but thinks like a novice. The expert will become confused and will have a problem as to the specificity of the replies. A second reason is that text books are notoriously poor at transmitting knowledge. Sometimes text books are quite wrong. More usually, they represent only a part of the required knowledge rather than a detailed explanation. Text books are written as part of a participatory course. Generally the text book is a contributory factor to the attainment of knowledge, in which most of the real learning is transmitted during face-to-face contact with a teacher. On its own or without the structure of the implied course, including discussions, practicals and the teacher's own experiences, the text book leads to more misunderstandings than knowledge. In most cases the working method of the expert is likely to be very different from a text book description. This is what makes the expert expert. The knowledge engineer may find he spends some of the first meeting deriding the particular approach taken by the authors of the text books. This is not a very fruitful way to spend time in the initial meetings. Text books may be useful, but take the expert's advice on which ones to read, if any. Be expert-led if you want to lead the expert.

If the knowledge engineer enters the first knowledge elicitation session with an open mind and an empty head his role is clear — he is the novice — more than that — the absolute novice. This is not a role he will have for long so it should be used wisely. It is at this time that the knowledge engineer can ask the most foolish of questions and say the silliest of things without irritating the expert. There is a human need to appear knowledgeable; the knowledge engineer has the perfect excuse to be totally ignorant.

The role of the knowledge engineer soon develops into that of an apprentice. As an apprentice the knowledge engineer may attempt to perform part of the expert's task; even if it is in a role playing situation or a teachback technique. In these situations the expert may become the client or an examiner. The fullest understanding is achieved by doing.

The role of the expert will also change. The expert will become, after a time, a part-time knowledge engineer. With a motivated expert this will happen automatically. It may even be necessary to devise strategies to hold the expert back from too close an involvement with the knowledge engineering, at least in the early stages. In later stages you will need all the help you can get from the expert. If that means the expert coding the knowledge in the knowledge representation language then, with good management, this is to be encouraged. It is possible, after all, that the maintenance of the system will be performed by the expert, so an early introduction to knowledge engineering will be vital. With a less motivated expert some subtle persuasion may be needed. Changing roles when the knowledge engineer acts the part of apprentice assists the expert's role change by forcing upon the expert a new part to play.

If text books are not recommended by the expert for familiarisation with the domain then familiarisation should be one of the first objectives of the orientation phase. A great deal of familiarisation takes place in what has been termed 'interview 1' (see the next chapter). A particularly useful strategy for familiarisation with the domain advocated by Regan (1986) is to identify the expert's psychological categories. This has the benefit of being directly useful in later analyses and possibly in implementation. The techniques for dealing with the elicitation of categorical knowledge is detailed below.

An objective of the orientation phase is the restriction of the scope of the investigation or the segmentation of the domain into separate phases of investigation. The first restriction or segment is by far the most important, as it is this area of knowledge which will become the basis of the knowledge used in the prototype system. The knowledge engineer must elicit that information which is relevant to taking this decision. He must assure himself that this sub-domain is as natural a division as possible. Remember: be expert-led — on this decision especially so. The prototype domain must be defined very clearly. It is likely that the knowledge engineering on this phase is the most difficult if only because of the limited knowledge held by the knowledge engineer. It is important that the task chosen for the prototype to perform is not too difficult, however, not too easy either. A task which is too easy to perform might not be an adequate examination of the domain or might not involve the participants to a satisfactory degree.

During knowledge elicitation the expert provides answers to questions or demonstrations of procedures. The answers take the form of factual information or explanations. It is the explanations that the knowledge engineer seeks and must comprehend. Although facts and descriptions are important, they are generally not controversial or difficult to understand. Explanations and justifications are the stock in trade of the knowledge engineer.

## THE STRUCTURE OF THE INTERVIEW

If an interview is to achieve its objectives it should be organised. Preparation is dealt with in chapter 7. However, part of the preparation takes place within the interview itself. The knowledge engineer should always have prepared an agenda. The interview should begin with a discussion of this agenda, and follow an agreed version of the agenda until some point where a digression seems more useful.

A byproduct of discussing the agenda is that the expert gains some knowledge concerning the knowledge engineer's current understanding of the domain. This may require the expert to perform some 'homework' to assist that understanding and thus may postpone a topic from the agenda. If the expert is to lead she must have information. The discussion of the agenda is a good time to impart that information.

The procedure adopted during the interview should have this very simple structure:
Evaluation of the replies and probing questions differs with the techniques the knowledge engineer is employing.

The duration of the interview should be until the agenda is exhausted — this is in fact unlikely as most interviews end when one of the participants becomes too fatigued to continue. Two hours of interviewing is close to the maximum for most individuals. Other techniques may have a longer or variable optimum duration. Observation, for example, may entail a day or longer if the expert's task is naturally of this duration. Observation should not be so tiring as interviewing, which for the inexperienced is surprisingly tiring. A break in the interview may revive the participants for another interview of shorter duration. The best procedure is to organise two interviews either side of lunch.

Discussion of the agenda is probably more important at the beginning of the knowledge acquisition phase. The same is true of the post-interview discussion. This discussion accompanied by the packing up of papers and the tape recorder focuses upon the interview rather than the domain. This gives the expert a chance to ask the knowledge engineer some questions concerning the knowledge engineering, the system, or to let off some steam. The expert may dislike or be irritated by a particular approach the knowledge engineer is using. If an alternative method which is less distasteful can be found then this must be an improvement. The post-interview discussion is one of the subtle ways in which the expert becomes involved in the knowledge engineering task as a knowledge engineer.

## THE TECHNIQUES

Following the approach used by Breuker and Wielinga (1983a), each of the techniques will be described and then greater detail will be provided in terms of the preconditions for using the technique, the objectives of using the technique and the particular problems which may be experienced.

### The focused interview

The focused interview is most similar to an ordinary conversation where one participant is interested in a topic of which the other participant is knowledgeable. Things are more structured in a knowledge elicitation session and usually follow a predetermined agenda. The agenda for interview 1, the major orientation interview, is presented in the next chapter.

Focused interviews, like any other interview, consist of asking a question from the agenda, assessing the reply and either probing for further information or if satisfied asking the next question from the agenda. The questions tend to be quite general, with instructions orientated to brief, broad replies. The focused interview is aimed at acquiring an overview of the domain and the task. The knowledge engineer may have to assert his control to keep the expert away from details at this time, with the reassurance that there will be an opportunity to discuss that particular topic in great detail

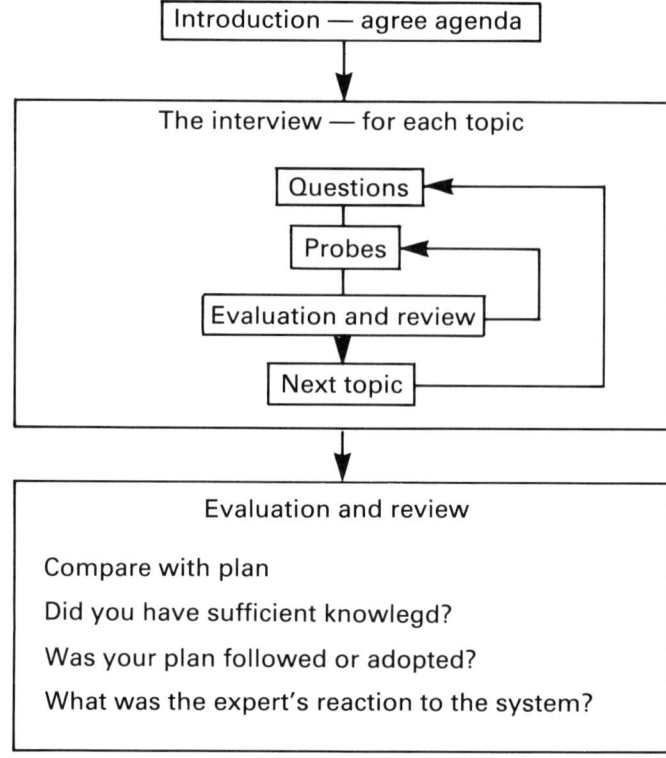

Fig. 5.1 — The structure of the interview.

later. The knowledge engineer may also remind the expert that he can only process so much information at any one time.

The objective of the focused interview is to obtain a complete overview of the domain. This should result in the compilation of an extensive glossary of technical terms and concepts relevant to that domain. The introductory interview, interview 1, is designed to achieve such an overview of the domain. Probes are used mainly to explicate the definitions of particular terms and concepts.

These early focused interviews will be set in the context of the feasibility study. The feasibility study should identify a possible sub-domain for a prototype implementation. The early interviews must investigate the type and characteristics of the expert's tasks without delving too deeply into the mechanics of the task itself. The questions for interview 1 (the task) are a guide as to how far the analysis needs to progress at the early stages of the project. These questions should cover most of the issues which need to be raised in the feasibility study but the knowledge engineer should always assume the list to be incomplete and attempt to generate questions which are domain specific. The task must be situated in the operational environment so a description of the role of the expertise in that environment can be made. The focused interview is ideal for obtaining a typology of objects and agents in the domain, basic factual knowledge and the characteristics of the expert's clients or potential users of the system.

As befits an initial technique, the preconditions which underlie the focused interview are the least demanding. The knowledge engineer must be prepared with at least an outline of which topics the interview will cover. A complete agenda, prepared in advance and sent to the expert, is preferable. If the knowledge engineer is very inexperienced in interviewing then it is advisable to obtain some practical experience first. The conversational nature of focused interviewing means motivation is unlikely to be a problem.

Breuker and Wielinga 83a suggest that a good knowledge of the specific domain vocabulary is necessary for focused interviewing. This begs the question as to where the knowledge engineer acquires the vocabulary. There would appear to be two readily available sources. Firstly, interview 1 will throw up many technical words which can form the basis of some of the later interviews. Secondly, some domains may be documented with text books or other source material which contain a glossary. If this is the case check this possible source with the expert before using it.

**Structured interviewing**
Structured interviewing resembles an interrogation rather than a conversation. Information is required at a much greater depth and specificity than in focused interviewing. The agenda takes the form of a list of subject headings rather than specific questions. The knowledge engineer is interested in covering these topics in detail, if possible, for the last time.

The expert should be informed as to the nature of the interview, that it constitutes a deeper inquiry into those areas or topics only briefly covered previously. Discussion of the order in which the topics should be taken, including whether they should be dealt with at this time, should precede the interview.

The structure of enquiry on each topic proceeds by a brief statement or a broad open question which details current understanding of the knowledge engineer and immediate information requirement. The expert should begin the discussion with an overview of the topic and perhaps without prompting begin a deeper analysis. The knowledge engineer requires the courage to interrupt even if the expert is in full flow. The discussion may have become far too complex for the knowledge engineer's current understanding, or a number of new or unfamiliar terms may have permeated the vocabulary. Whatever the reason for interrupting, it must be done with tact and resolution. Such interjections as 'Now if I can just stop you there and . . .' or 'I'm sorry but I'll have to interrupt before we get too deep and . . .' are adequate. Remember if you do interrupt it is better to give the reason why.

As the investigation of one particular topic progresses, the number of closed questions and probes requiring short answers increases. The knowledge engineer should not expect to cover all of the details at the first attempt. It is preferable to progress only so far as the knowledge engineer's current understanding and the expert's powers of explanation will allow.

For a successful detailed investigation of a domain there is a requirement for more than just a basic knowledge of the domain. Hence, structured interviewing follows on from focused interviewing, general knowledge acquisition (this includes studying glossaries, case studies and text books) and analysis. A precursor to beginning a number of structured interviews is a knowledge review. This is the technique by which the knowledge engineer verifies his understanding of the domain. The technique is described below.

Other preconditions for the use of structured interviewing are good interviewing skills and ability to control the interview. The demands of the structured interview are considerably increased in comparison to the focused interview. This will require the expert to be more motivated. Forewarning the expert as to the possible troubles which may be encountered can only defuse the problems which lie ahead. A debriefing session may also smooth this difficult path to enlightenment.

The main purpose of the structured interview is to obtain a deeper insight into the structure of the domain objects and their relationships. Focused interviews will have discovered the facts that particular loans are made to a particular business in particular circumstances. For example, the knowledge engineer discovers, during a focused interview, that the finance a company needs is dependent upon the sort of company it is, the business it is involved in and other circumstances. During a structured interview the question, which company gets what finance and in what circumstances, requires a mass of detail. The focus of attention may shift from finance to different methods of categorising companies, then to all the different indices that describe the state of the financial world. It is details that count. A knowledge-base is a store of detail organised with respect to an overt information processing strategy (the expert's method). The focused interviews show the knowledge engineer the way, the focused interviews provide him with the details; and the various methods of task analysis provide the information processing strategy.

During structured interviewing the knowledge engineer elicits explanations and justifications for particular sub-tasks and thus increases his own understanding in advance of a detailed task analysis. Knowledge engineers are warned not to progress to attempting an analysis of the task without a very good understanding of the static aspects of the domain. The static aspects of the domain include the never-changing indisputable facts, theories and conceptual objects. The dynamic aspects of the domain are concerned with the actual performance of the task and more specifically with the reasoning processes which guide the expert throughout that performance.

**Probes**
The **addition probe** encourages the expert to provide more information by simply making it understood that what has been said has been understood. Either verbally or non-verbally the message is, 'Go on tell me more', 'Don't

stop'. This probe is most likely to be used in the initial stages of knowledge elicitation during a structured interview when a new topic is first raised. At this time the knowledge engineer is seeking breadth and a basic understanding of the subject matter, and any further information which the expert is willing to impart is gratefully received.

The **reflecting probe**, by using a non-directive technique, encourages the expert to go deeper into the topic. This probe should be used when the expert's current response tails off and the account still remains incomplete. If the expert looks as if she is not prepared to continue, the knowledge engineer could restate a synthesis of the expert's response as a proposition. This type of probe is more likely to be of use during focused interviewing when the expert is not contributing as much as the knowledge engineer would like or during structured interviewing when the knowledge engineer does not have enough information to use a more investigative probe.

The **directive probe** specifies the direction in which a continuation of the reply should follow without suggesting any particular content. The expert may have given a list of possible statuses which an object can take during some process. The knowledge engineer asks for detail on the nature of each change and thus requests more specificity from the expert. If the expert gives a reply which is judged too specific then a directive probe may be used to shift the emphasis to more general comments. Such a probe may take the form of, 'why is that (the case)?'. A directive probe may be used to shift the emphasis of information in either a focused or structured interview.

The **change of mode probe** is used to provide another point of view. After describing a particular aspect from a theoretical perspective the knowledge engineer may ask what the implications are from a methodological point of view. Alternative change of modes would include moving from abstract or general examples to the specific or looking at the functionality of objects rather than their descriptive characteristics or category membership. Change of mode probes should be used during structured interviewing when the knowledge engineer has gained a greater familiarity with the domain so changes of mode are contextually meaningful.

The **defining probe** requires the expert to explain the meaning of a particular term or concept. In order to sustain a steady progress through the agenda these defining probes may be held back to the beginning of the next interview. However, this may mean that the analysis of the interview is hampered. If much of the current interview is postponed to later interviews then this will not be such a problem.

### Self report and think aloud protocols

The think aloud protocol has been widely used by knowledge engineers. It is a technique borrowed directly from cognitive psychology where it has been used to investigate reasoning strategies while solving problems. The problems solved by subjects in a cognitive psychology experiment tend to be artificial and/or simple. Experts are experts largely because they are able to solve complex problems which others cannot. This is the essential difficulty in justifying the use of the think aloud technique in knowledge engineering.

Nevertheless, think-aloud protocols may be used effectively if some thought is given to the particular problems which affect knowledge elicitation.

The very complexity of the expert's task will require the task to be segmented into manageable proportions. The exact delineations of a task can be discovered by attempting a think aloud protocol on the whole task with the purpose of discovering the natural breaks. The expert is then asked to perform as she normally would, the only difference being that a running commentary is given. The knowledge engineer may need to prompt the expert if there is an extended silence. Otherwise, the knowledge engineer's only other duty is to monitor any recording equipment which is being used and make notes of any points which need to be resolved as soon as the task is complete. It may be necessary to ask the expert to perform the same task or similar tasks more than once.

It is very unlikely that the expert will have any experience in talking while doing her job, so it may be advisable to consider a number of training sessions. The optimum performance is where the expert is unconscious of talking and is able to perform the task as if she was silent. This will be an optimum that will probably never be achieved, although the opposite occurrence where the expert forgets to talk but performs the task perfectly is very common. The author has heard of an expert who was so frustrated by this process that she excused herself for a short while so she could solve the problem in some privacy. The greatest danger with this technique is the strong possibility that the requirement for detailed expression directed at a novice will interfere substantially with the performance. The expert may well find talking and doing difficult and thus the knowledge engineer is put in a position of prompting someone who is in difficulties or allowing a period of silent reflection to take place and possibly losing a lot of useful data.

Problems notwithstanding, the knowledge engineer should attempt a think aloud protocol to elicit detailed information concerning the task with the purpose of obtaining information on the sequencing and structure of sub-tasks. The expert's rules of thumb will be expressed but only in a piecemeal fashion. A full catalogue of these heuristics will require a number of think aloud protocols to be run with the corresponding likelihood of much duplication. It is important for the knowledge engineer to inform the expert that he is not concerned with 'book' knowledge but the way the expert 'actually' performs the task. There may be a conflict between organisational directives as how to perform the task and the way the expert actually does it. The knowledge engineer will have to decide, with the expert's guidance, as to which procedure to implement in the final system. It is preferable to simulate the expert's actual practice.

The reasoning strategies which the expert uses to perform her task have to be inferred from the think aloud data by the knowledge engineer. The reasoning strategies implemented in the system may well be determined by the programming environment. The use of an expert system shell may limit the knowledge engineer's options. Many shells are based on production rules which can seriously reduce the ability to model subtle reasoning processes. More flexibility is conferred by using computer languages such as

PROLOG or LISP, although the trade-off is greater representational power against more complex programming tasks. The knowledge engineer should be aware of system constraints and how they are likely to affect the knowledge acquisition phase.

The knowledge engineer uses the information provided by think aloud protocols as the subject matter for structured interviews with special emphasis on the implementation of the reasoning strategies. This is assisted by the knowledge engineer mentally taking the role of the expert system. Taking the role of the system requires the knowledge engineer to imagine how he (the computer) would perform the task. The knowledge engineer requires some knowledge of what structures exist and what types of processing are available in the expert system's knowledge representation language. He may not be required to implement the finished system himself so knowledge of actual implementation techniques are not important.

The think aloud protocol techniques are useful in providing those processes by which the expert evaluates progress, information vital for the control of the simulation. Verification of the evaluative criteria of the expert should be carried out as a matter of urgency. Analysis of think aloud protocols reveals the structure of the task. This technique is a supplement to other techniques, especially structured interviews concerned with the task.

The first tasks which the expert performs while talking are chosen for their ease and usefulness in extracting the structure of the sub-tasks. This is very much a training period for the expert so any extra information is a bonus. The choice of later tasks should be related to the test cases or constitute part of the test case suite. Test cases are the body of tasks which are used to check the development of the implementation of the system. They also perform a useful role in the knowledge acquisition process as the subject matter of think aloud protocols and interviews. The criteria for selection of both test cases and the think aloud problems are very similar. Common sense suggests that they should be combined while the efficacy of performing think aloud protocols is high. A test case or subject of a think aloud protocol should be typical of the tasks which the expert usually performs. If the task is a simulation then the parameters or components of the problem should be indistinguishable from an actual problem. The content of the problem should not be too difficult or too easy but should provide some challenge to the expert. The solution should fall into a common class of solutions and should not be overly elegant or creative, or one which would be beyond the scope of a fairly unrefined knowledge-base to handle.

A number of variations of the think aloud technique may be attempted if the 'tell all' variation is too demanding or has lost some of its efficacy by virtue of repetition of what has become well understood information.

The **critical response method** requires the expert to be vocal only when one or more specially identified sub-tasks are being performed. The expert should begin the report by setting the scene — where the report of the reasoning process begins.

This last point is central to the technique known as **periodic report**. This technique is used if the task is very complex and the expert has had difficulty thinking aloud and performing the task at the same time. The knowledge engineer and the expert agree on a particular time interval. When the allotted time has passed the expert is duty bound to report what she is currently trying to achieve and what steps have led to that situation. An attempt should be made to achieve the continuity from one report to the next. When the report is complete the expert collects her thoughts and continues until it is time to report again. The interval depends upon the complexity of the task with shorter intervals for more complex tasks, and vice versa. This technique is very time-consuming and quite tiring. There is a possibility that the expert will not complete the whole task in the allotted time so it may be preferable to use the periodic report method with a subdivision of the task.

**Report by commentary** is a more relaxed method if the requisite stimulus materials exist. The expert is given some form of stimulus material such as an audio or video tape of the task being performed (preferably by herself) and her comments are recorded. Wood (1986) has used training videos which demonstrate a task being performed badly. This is an interesting alternative which prompts the expert to identify the errors of the novice and thereby elicits the correct method. A computer printout or documentary evidence may perform the same function if the task is either silent or inactive.

The knowledge engineer should attempt to obtain these artifacts as a matter of course irrespective of whether he intends to record the expert's comments. Real life recordings or task artifacts provide much information even without an expert commentary.

If it is possible to record the interaction between expert and client then this should be attempted. The dialogue presents a good source of information for further interviews and gives the knowledge engineer an idea of the client's role in the expert process. If the system is to be used by the client, the recording supplies useful background information in order to plan the detailed interviews with the projected users of the system.

Focused and structured interviewing and think aloud techniques represent the most useful and widely used methods to elicit expert knowledge. The rest of the techniques reviewed in this chapter are of minor use. However, the first — the **repertory grid technique** — is regarded by some as a very powerful knowledge elicitation method.

## REPERTORY GRIDS

The repertory grid technique was developed by the psychologist Kelly (1955) as a method of eliciting the structure of human thinking as described by his personal construct theory. Kelly argued that an individual's way of perceiving the world was unique. An understanding of how a person sees his world must be based on the concepts he uses to describe and differentiate between significant objects. Any investigation must begin by explicating those concepts or constructs. The repertory grid technique is used to extract an individual's constructs and then apply them to all the significant objects in the individual's world. The psychologist begins by asking the Subject (the capital S denotes a human subject of a psychological experiment) to list a number of significant objects. Somewhere between ten and twenty would be adequate. Then randomly drawing three objects from the list the Subject identifies which two of the three are most alike and which one is the most dissimilar. The Subject then identifies the construct underlying this discrimination. This process is repeated until a reasonable number of constructs have been elicited. Then each object is rated as to its position on a bipolar scale for each construct. A statistical analysis such as factor analysis is used to compare the objects in the grid.

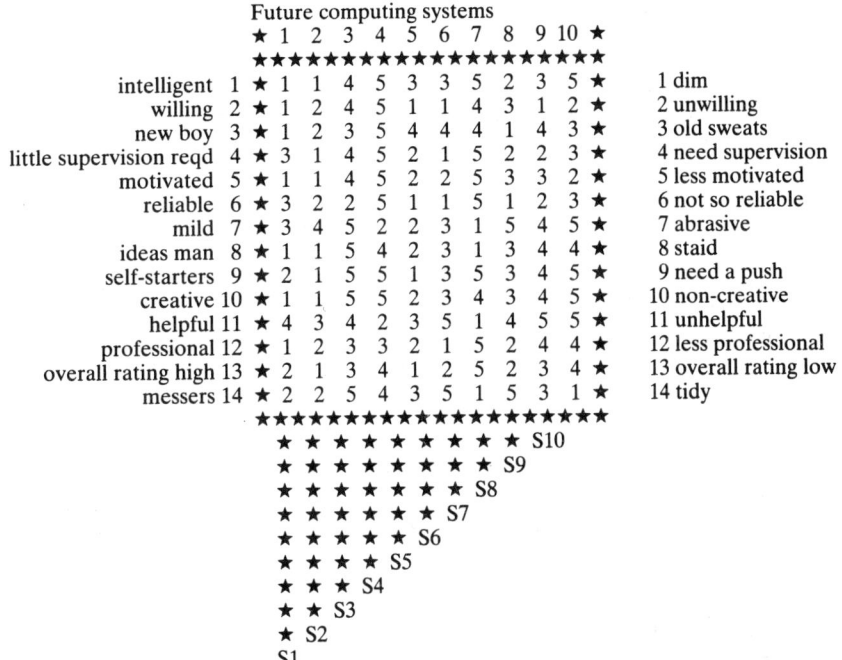

Fig. 5.2 — PEGASUS: repertory grid elicited on staff appraisal. (From Mildred L. G. Shaw and Brian R. Gaines: "Interactive elicitation of knowledge from experts". *Future Computing Systems*, **1** (2) (1986).)

Repertory grids were used by Kelly so his Subjects could reveal indirectly any subjective beliefs or feelings which may be embarrassing or threatening, and therefore quite difficult to reveal directly. Also, Subjects discovered a clear representation of their world described in their own terms which, quite often, came as something as a surprise for them. Using the technique to elicit objective knowledge is a departure from its initial use. The effect of any technique of knowledge elicitation cannot be entirely predicted. This is also true of interviewing and think aloud protocols. However, as a guide, those techniques that resemble everyday activities, such as talking and explaining, or which approximate to the actual task will be the least likely to create artifacts. The repertory grid technique will probably be new to the expert and unlike anything she has had experience of before. This may reduce her participation. However, the rather special status of knowledge engineer, as someone who uses strange methods, does mililate against the expert's adverse reaction. If the knowledge engineer has previously explained that he has a bag of methods some of which the expert will have never seen before, then the repertory grid technique will be given a fair trial by the expert. The knowledge engineer should be aware, however, that the imposition of alien techniques upon the expert may cause some unwelcome effects.

There is some dispute over the utility of the data which is derived from the repertory grid technique. With most expert domains there is likely to be a moderately large number of objects. This may generate an even larger number of constructs. Only the expert will be able to discriminate between those constructs which have a limited use and those which have an important function in the domain. Statistical analysis of the results seems to have a limited utility too. It is the meaning, use and structure of an object or concept, in that order, which are important. The degree of similarity between concepts is rarely useful unless the system requires such knowledge of similarity. When other authors have attempted to extol the virtues of repertory grids they have used rather simplistic domains for their analysis. Hart (1986) looks at musical instruments and finds that a trumpet is more like a clarinet than a drum! In the author's experience and opinion it is difficult to envisage how a domain analysis would benefit more from the repertory technique than from a structured and systematic interviewing schedule. In fact it would appear that the analysis has benefited from discussion, debate and of course audio recording. Elicitation within an interview setting allows the participants to judge what is important and what is not while the topic is under discussion. Experience seems to suggest that a knowlege engineer with good interview technique (it does not have to be very good) is better than a dubious psychology technique.

Rather than follow the repertory grid technique as presented above, adaptations may be used which move the technique closer to an interviewing format. Identification of the significant objects is a necessary step in creating the domain glossary. To achieve this, the knowledge engineer may run a small repertory grid to demonstrate the technique and largely ignore the results. The knowledge engineer explains what is expected and asks the expert for her opinion on how the technique might be best used — remember: be expert-led — then runs the technique to expose the major constructs in the domain and how they are related to the major categories of objects in the domain. An alternative or subsequent variation would be to segment the domain along some fairly natural lines and apply the technique to significant objects in each sub-domain. Hart(1986) has suggested that the repertory grid technique should be used as an orientation to the domain. This would appear to be an error in understanding the structure of the domain, and a fairly good grasp of the terminology seems to represent the basic preconditions for using the repertory grid technique.

Kelly intended the repertory grid technique to allow the Subjects to understand their own personalities by describing their world in their own terms. The psychologist was not expected to understand the Subject's repertory grid in the same way as the Subject did. To do that, the psychologist must understand what each construct means to the Subject. The utility of the repertory technique is increased by the foreknowledge of the domain. Probably the most important use of the repertory grid technique in knowledge engineering is to create data for structured interviews. A discussion of each construct, how it is applied, its relationship to other objects and any theoretical issues will provide much useful information.

The ease of programming this technique has led some (Shaw and Gaines, 1986) to suggest its use in automatic rule generation and hence automatic knowledge acquisition. The current work in this area does seem to support the claim made in this book that the discussion of the data derived from repertory grids provides more insights than the statistical analysis of it. Repertory grid technique is of most use when the expert is having difficulty expressing the information or is generally inarticulate. The technique is less useful for experts who are capable of explaining concepts well during interviews. Properly managed interviews should always be the most efficient method of eliciting information.

**Forward scenario simulation**

**Forward scenario simulation** provides a bridge from structured interviewing to think aloud protocols. The technique requires the expert to take a verbal walk through the reasoning processes used to complete the expert task. As this is an interview rather than a report on an actual performance of the task, there is the possibility of a shallow description resulting. The method depends upon uncued memory recall which cannot be relied upon and is susceptible to distortion, in particular post hoc rationalisation. Recall is always more accurate when cues are presented.

There are a number of other difficulties associated with this method. Firstly, the expert may use a number of terms which are unfamiliar to the knowledge engineer. Requesting the definitions of these terms will interrupt the flow of the commentary. Allowing the monologue to continue runs the risk that the description of the process will not be fully understood. It is probably advisable to interrupt. That way at least an entry into the domain glossary is achieved.

The second difficulty is associated with the narrowness of the reasoning path. The majority of the number of 'ifs . . .', 'however,. . .' and 'this also might be the case . . .' are ignored by the expert. However, using this technique to bridge the gap between interviewing (static domain analysis) and think aloud protocols (dynamic task analysis) turns a problem into a bonus. Paradoxically, too specific a description is more likely to cause the knowledge engineer problems. The knowledge engineer needs simple descriptions of the task, avoiding any problems and complexities. A simple description of the task translates into the basic expert method which is used as a first attempt at implementation. Anything more complex than a fairly simplistic form of the expert's method would be wasted. Advising the expert as to the level of specificity explicitly avoids a too detailed and too shallow commentary.

The third difficulty is in distinguishing between the expert's reasoning methods and the actual task itself. Reasoning is an abstraction, cognitive and not the material for recall. The processes which underpin the overt performance of a task are not described as such. The expert does not say, '... at this point I construct a hypothesis which I will test against the evidence ...' and yet this may be the form of reasoning model which the knowledge engineer is trying to construct. As with think aloud protocols and observation, the knowledge engineer must induce what reasoning strategies lie behind the performance or description of the performance. It is the expert's job to explain as clearly as possible what they do and how they do it; the knowledge engineer is there to translate that description into a model of the reasoning processes.

**Goal decomposition**
The **goal decomposition technique** requires the expert to describe a reasoning process analogous to the expert system rule firing strategy of backward chaining. The knowledge engineer provides the expert with a conclusion or goal and the expert describes what tasks must have been performed or conditions satisfied in order to have reached that state. In essence the expert strives to reduce a problem into sub-problems. This elicitation strategy may be especially useful if the control structure of the expert system utilises backward chaining.

The purpose of this method is to attain some quite specific task information. One problem is where to place it in the knowledge acquisition phase. A strong precondition is a good understanding of the task, and this suggests that the technique should be used after forward scenario simulation or in conjunction with think aloud protocols.

The expert may find this an alien technique, so there is a risk of eliciting artificial information. As with forward scenario simulation, the ability to explore the task space may be a problem if there are many alternatives to achieving a desired goal. If this is the case it is unlikely that goal decomposition will be an efficient method of knowledge elicitation.

**Inqusitive observatiuon**
This refers to a type of observation in which the expert performs the task in the actual setting or a setting as realistic as possible, while the knowledge engineer interrupts at various times asking why a particular action or choice was made. This has the effect of breaking the natural flow of reasoning. The knowledge engineer is advised to make a special attempt to remember where the expert had got to before the interruption.

This technique avoids the difficulty of having to comment on every stage associated with the think aloud protocol methods but supplies much less information. It is advisable that the knowledge engineer should have a very good knowledge of the task before using this technique. The technique is probably best used to achieve a fuller understanding of the fine details of the task.

Inquisitive observation turns the expert's task into a resource which generates topics for discussion. Quite simply, the knowledge engineer observes in silence until something happens which prompts him to interrupt and clear up the confusion. The type of interviewing technique is undoubtedly focused, as the required information will most probably be very specific. The questions the knowledge engineer asks must be heavily constrained by instructions as to the sort of answer required. Typically these instructions detail the knowledge engineer's perceived confusion and the knowledge which is being used to realise what the nature of this confusion is. The expert then has a choice of providing the information which the knowledge engineer lacked or correcting the mistaken assumption which prompted the interruption.

**Classification**

An important element of any domain of expertise is the classification structure used by the experts. Techniques which elicit this structure are very useful in the orientation phase of knowledge acquisition. The repertory grid is one technique which can be utilised to this end. Another method is to represent the domain objects listed by the expert on cards. The expert is then asked to order or arrange these cards whatever way she feels. There may well be many different configurations so the knowledge engineer is recommended to perform the exercise on an empty desk and then take photographs of the results. This method has the advantage of providing some very powerful stimulus material for future interviews and diagrammatic reference material for the knowledge engineer's documentation set.

Once the salient categories have been identified, the knowledge engineer shifts attention to the definition of stereotypes, that is, objects that represent typical members of a category. A structured interview should follow this initial stage to identify the categorical heuristics. The enquiry should focus upon which attributes entities need to be considered for membership of a category and which attributes debar an entity from membership. The knowledge engineer induces from the information a structure of the domain objects. He is, then, advised to present a schematic representation of this analysis to the expert. The structure of domain objects is domain specific. An example may be found in the final chapter. However, it must be noted that those examples were created by the knowledge engineers on the basis of focused and structured interviews without the assistance of any classificational techniques.

Identification of category structures leads to an understanding of the domain, but it is not, unless the role of the system is categorisation, directly relevant to implementation. However, classification may feature in the stage of defining the task parameters. A category structure may also be used as the basis of the object structure in the knowledge-base if the implementation is object orientated.

### Systematic symptom-to-fault links

The stimulus material for this particular technique of knowledge elicitation is a list of all possible faults or problems and possible symptoms. The expert is then asked to describe the relationship between the faults and the symptoms. An obvious extension is for the expert to include information on possible solutions or actions which can be taken in these hypothetical conditions.

The purpose of this strategy is to build a coherent structure of the relationship between problem, symptom and solution directly under the expert's guidance. A good understanding of the domain and the task structure is a precondition for using this strategy.

### Decision elicitation

Chapter 2 contained a description of the bare bones of a methodology based upon an analysis of expertise into psychological and behavioural components. In the realms of the psychological, the knowledge engineer is recommended to take account of the decision making behaviour of the expert. What follows is a technique which formalises the elicitation of decision making behaviour.

Firstly, we must be certain that a decision is being made rather than a script being followed. This fairly trivial step is followed by the close scrutiny of the decision making environment. The knowledge engineer is interested in a complete description of that situation — when it happens, what the values of particular parameters are and what the likely outcomes of alternative decisions would be. A full description of the decision situation can be formulated as a list of significant attributes and the likely values of these attributes. Values may be specific, within a range, unknown or inferred. Accompanying these values is a certainty that that value would hold for all situations.

Decisions are made so that circumstances change. The knowledge engineer now shifts his attention to the possible outcomes of this particular decision and what the determinants of these outcomes are. The knowledge engineer must document which facts are relevant (determinants) at the time the decision is taken and outcome decided.

To sum up, define the significant objects in the domain of judgemental behaviour, those objects which constitute the situation in which judgemental behaviour takes place. This situation is characterised by an array of attributes with corresponding values. Judgemental behaviour itself is represented by the choice of one decision from a matrix of applicable decisions. With each decision there exists a number of possible outcomes, each one with a likely probability. The subjective nature of the domain of judgemental behaviour cannot be over emphasised. It is the knowledge engineer's main task to build a bridge between the subjectivity of the expert's responses and the objectivity demanded by a knowledge representation formalism.

Finally, at the subjective extreme there exists the knowledge states of the expert. These consist of relevant facts which are known in advance and used by the expert to reach the right decision. When all the information has been collected, analysed and documented — look for the rules and heuristics which underpin the behaviour. As this may be very complex, work from the simplest cases first.

**Analytical behaviour elicitation**
Analysis is that process which reduces or otherwise alters a formalism in order to make the informational content held within the formalism clearer, usually at the expense of a more complex and somewhat esoteric formalism. What this means is that one representation of information is turned into a second, probably more oblique, representation, which is more amenable to interpretation from a particular context. A clear example of this is the statistical analysis of a set of examination results so that raw scores are turned into z-scores using the standard deviation of the raw scores in order that comparisons can be made between the same candidates across different subjects. Analysis is not always as explicit as the previous example. The knowledge engineer is interested in the internal (i.e. mental) analysis techniques of the expert. Not only are these types of analysis internal: they may also be internalised, which will make elicitation difficult.

The elicitation of judgemental behaviour begins with a description of the situation within which the behaviour occurred. The elicitation of analysis techniques begins with a description of the object or formalism to be transformed. Whereas with judgemental behaviour we are interested in the situation in terms of the attributes and values, with analysis the objects must be described in terms of a structure consisting of parts and relationships.

Secondly, the original formalism must be described in whatever way is applicable — the expert's description is usually the best. Thirdly, the derived formalism is described, preferably in a way similar to the original formalism. Fourthly, the object of the analysis, that is, the purpose in terms of the meaning or information which may be interpreted from the second formalism, is sought. Lastly, the process of transformation between the two formalisms is described and documented, firstly as a script and then in a suitable intermediate representation (see chapter 8 for information on intermediate representations). The most important point is that the knowledge engineer should understand the analytical process as well as document it.

**Review**
This is not really a knowledge elicitation strategy but a necessary verification procedure. The knowledge engineer must from time to time present to the expert a collection of propositions gleaned from prior interviews and other sources. This should be presented as a numbered list and discussed in terms of the proposition's veracity and applicability. Some of these propositions may be true but have such a tenuous relationship to the defined domain that any further investigation can be curtailed. It is often the case that the knowledge engineer finds some area of the domain to be interesting from a personal point of view and requests more information irrespective of its utility to the proposed system. This is more likely if the knowledge engineer

has some background in the domain, prior to the knowledge acquisition sessions. The analysis of the review interview is used to complete an elicitation phase on a subset of the domain prior to implementation.

The knowledge engineer is advised to follow a review with an initial sortie into the next phase of the knowledge engineering at the same interview. This provides data for planning interviews relating to the next section of the knowledge-base.

**Teachback**

Review is one technique of knowledge validation — **teachback** is another. The term is self-explanatory, and in its simplest form the technique consists of the knowledge engineer playing the role of the expert and explaining some concept or the reasoning behind a particular process. A more dynamic variant of teachback consists of the knowledge engineer performing a simulation of the expert task. This should not be attempted until the knowledge engineer and the expert consider that the knowledge engineer has a good understanding of the task. Secondly, the task should be a realistic simulation but without too many problems or difficulties. If teachback can be combined with a deeper understanding of the test cases then this is an added bonus. Thirdly, the expert should, at least initially, be on hand to guide the knowledge engineer. The knowledge engineer is, in effect, put in the position of performing a think aloud protocol. This gives him a chance to find out what it feels like from the other side. The think aloud technique is important; otherwise he may perform the right action for the wrong reason.

The attempt to perform the task has the effect of uncovering a lot of the ambiguities and misunderstandings that the knowledge engineer was only dimly aware of. Depending upon the time available to perform the task, the knowledge engineer should preferably have several attempts until he becomes reasonably adept. At this stage it might be possible to dispense with the expert's assistance in helping the knowledge engineer perform the task (this will reduce some of the costs of knowledge elicitation) and use the knowledge engineer's attempts to emulate an expert as a source of subject matter for interviews or to structure an interrogative observation session with the expert. Once the knowledge engineer can do some of the expert's tasks he can explore the area for himself and return to the expert when he is lost or for a validation exercise.

During the task the knowledge engineer should play the role of the prospective system, always asking himself how the system can emulate (or preferably simulate) this particular procedure. There is an important input to the design from this exercise. It can only come from the knowledge engineer and it should not be wasted. Teachback does not only provide important validation but a clearer understanding of the implementational issues.

Teachback should not be regurgitation of the facts. Facts are not interesting in their own right. The place for facts is in the relative document. Teachback is about demonstrating an understanding in a dynamic context.

**The translator**
Some experts are very scarce and/or their expertise is very esoteric. If the expertise is very esoteric it would take the knowledge engineer too long to learn the basics in the domain and this would be prohibitively expensive. The expense of eliciting knowledge from a very scarce source is also a disincentive for the project to continue. A solution is to find a less expert but proficient individual who understands enough knowledge engineering concepts to assist with the knowledge acquisition phase of the project. This individual then takes the role of knowledge engineer's assistant and acts as a technical translator. This team approach dramatically reduces the time the expert will be required.

## TECHNIQUES FOR DEALING WITH MULTIPLE EXPERTS

An expert system project is as likely to bring together the expertise of a number of individuals as it is to focus upon the expertise of one single person. Even where only one expert is required as a source of the relevant expertise it may be possible to draw upon the assistance of a pool of experts. The use of a pool of roughly equivalent experts gives the knowledge engineer more access to the expertise assuming they are not too concerned with which actual individual they will be working with. Alternatively, a combination of expertise from a number of individuals and other sources may be the only way possible to achieve the functionality of the system. This type of system will be referred to as an expert synthesis system.

Generally, it is advisable to work with one expert with respect to knowledge elicitation and employ the talents of any others to test and suggest changes to the system. Concentrating upon one expert for the overwhelming majority of the knowledge is contingent upon her having all the required expertise with the competence for transferring that expertise, being available for the interviews and any other meetings (with the intended users for example). In other words the expert must be highly motivated and prepared to take a dominant role in the development of system. This high degree of commitment is usually found only when the system was originally suggested by the expert or she has other very important reasons for seeing the project to a successful conclusion. If the full commitment of a single expert cannot be guaranteed then the use of a limited number of less experienced experts is an alternative, with the aim of concentrating upon one or two who have the commitment and are able to perform well in knowledge elicitation sessions.

The problem of multiple-expert projects is largely a problem of project management than one which requires any major changes to the knowledge engineering techniques. The problems are largely concerned with communication and responsibility. With more than one expert contributing to the project the knowledge engineer must take a more dominant and more central role in the project management. The logistics of the project become far more complex with a number of experts making different contributions. Just getting three experts in the same room at the same time, sharing the same information can be surprisingly difficult. A project which relies upon contributions from a number of experts is less flexible than one which relies upon a single expert. There is a tendency to plan further ahead — taking into account the problem of scheduling meetings with a number of busy people. Changing the project or knowledge engineering plan may result in delays if new knowledge elicitation sessions have to be re-arranged. The knowledge engineer can ease the managerial problems by getting the expert's to do 'home work' and bring the results of this, such as a pencil and paper draft knowledge-base, to the meetings for detailed discussion. Within a methodology based on understanding it is as important that the expert understands the knowledge engineer's requirements as it is for the knowledge engineer to understand the knowledge engineering capabilities of the expert. Hence the need for good communications amongst all the participants.

The nature of expertise is such, that different approaches, usually only at the level of emphasis, are taken to similar tasks and problems. It is in the nature of human experts that heated differences of opinion can arise over these seemingly trivial points. The solution as previously stated is to appoint one expert as the 'knowledge Czar (or Czarina)'. This refers to her role as the final arbiter. The obvious choice is the expert with the most power and experience in the organisation. Often the expert who is ideal for participating in the knowledge elicitation sessions, by being the most experienced, is the one with the least availability. However, the role of final arbiter is one which such an expert can take without committing herself to an uncontrollable amount of work.

A major advantage of using multiple experts, where the overlap between each person's expertise is high, is the number of alternative solutions and perspectives which can be generated either in a group situation or while working singly with the knowledge engineer. Where there is a significant degree of divergence in the methods and/or knowledge used by the experts, the disparity between the alternative perspectives will be greater. In this case then some experts may only be of marginal use as a greater role would lead to problems when attempting to integrate the contributions from all the experts. The scope of each of the possible contributors must be identified as part of the feasibility phase of the project, that is, as a definitive goal of the individual domain analyses. An extra role for the feasibility study is to define the roles of each expert within the multi-expert project.

An alternative to the expert simulation system is the expert synthesis system. This variety of expert system combines the expertise of a number of individuals from probably quite diverse fields. An expert synthesis system is an artificially intelligent system with the role of the unique expert in a hypothetical or constructed domain. This must be one of the most difficult computing projects at the present time. The use of a number of experts with divergent expertise necessitates a multiple domain analysis to clearly delineate the limits of each domain. A corresponding analysis should take place with the proposers of the system in order to gain a clear idea of the hypothetical combinative domain. Systems of this complexity need a more complex methodology. One methodology being developed at the time of writing falls under the title of requirements analysis (Barthelemy *et al.*, 1987). This approach aims to develop an expert system by basing the design on a detailed enquiry into the requirements for that system. This is an attempt to orient the methodology towards the user's real needs and away from the knowledge engineer's prejudices and the expert's method. The approach is applicable to expert simulation systems too, but its rigorous attention to detail make it ideal for synthetic systems.

Involving the user at an early stage is vital. The user's knowledge and experience have a direct bearing on the type of system which it is possible to construct with respect to usability and acceptance. The knowledge elicitation techniques used for a multi-expert system are very similar to the domain analysis carried out with a single expert and described in this chapter. Where differences tend to show up is in the detailed analysis work which must take place when attempting to understand the broad outlines of the domain. A greater emphasis is placed on the analysis of the system's functionality as seen by the proposer of the system, which includes identifying the overlaps between the experts. As a priority those areas of system functionality which require combinations from two experts should be identified. Apart from where knowledge can be taken directly from one person the combination of the knowledge of two experts offers the least potential problems and should be tackled before those areas which require the input of more than two domain experts.

The management of multi-expert synthesis systems should proceed from a domain analysis with the individual experts and be followed by more detailed knowledge elicitation still with individual experts. As a precursor to focused interviewing, a brainstorming session should be attempted. The goal of this session is to define the synthetic domain and should involve the experts, users, any other interested parties and of course the knowledge engineering team. A brainstorming session as a part of the feasibility study is highly recommended, and of course, it may be useful to hold a second brainstorming session with the feasibility report as an major item of discussion and preceding the focused interviews with the different experts. Much useful information will be generated from the discussions during the brainstorming sessions and should be documented for possible use later in the project. A well documented and well presented account of the meeting can make for an impressive deliverable to senior management. One problem with expert synthesis systems is the slow progress and lack of deliverables, particularly software, in the preliminary and first cut phases. The report of the brainstorming sessions will lessen the disquiet which senior management feel owing to the slow progress.

A by-product of the brainstorming session which may be of greater use than any knowledge-based findings is the assessment of the personalities of the contributors with respect to working in a group situation. Any likely personality clashes between two participants or individuals who exhibit less than welcome personality traits, aggressive behaviour or acute shyness should be noted.

The completion of the knowledge analysis from the individual experts, including review or teachback, should be followed by elicitation sessions involving dyads. Two factors influence the choice of which experts and which combination of domain is chosen for the first investigations. Firstly, and in this the knowledge engineer should be guided by the feasibility report, the development of the first cut prototype should take precedence over other considerations. The second factor influencing the choice of which domains of expertise are merged is the likely degree of difficulty in bringing together the two domains. The calculation of the degree of difficulty must take into account the personalities of the experts and how these might interact during the knowledge elicitation session. If the experts' personalities do not pose a problem then the difficulty of combining two domains is determined by the closeness of the two domains such as the number of terms in common, the shared theories and methods. The source of this information is the same source for the feasibility study. The ideal combination of experts in the first cut phase should offer a not too difficult challenge to the participants, follow on logically from the focused interviews, involve two experts who can work together and produce a result which contributes directly to the first cut prototype.

McGraw and Seale (1988) is one of the few papers which has covered in any detail the problems of multi-expert projects. They recommend a number of techniques which they suggest should be used to elicit knowledge during a multi-expert project.

One of the issues Mcgraw and Seale regard as important is the difference between group and individual judgement. Small group judgement tends to be better than individual judgement and offers the possibility of selecting the optimum solution to a set problem (Steiner, 1972; Slater, 1958). This is an important finding with respect to the elicitation of test cases. The elicitation, and even the formulation, of test cases will be difficult when the expertise is widely distributed amongst a number of individuals. It is vital, therefore, to combine the relevant knowledge from the experts with regard to the identification, selection and detailed analysis of the test cases. McGraw and Seale recommend that no more than three experts are used in the problem solving groups. However, practical constraints and the actual definition of the hypothetical domain may require more individuals to combine their problem solving skills and specific knowledge. The knowledge engineer should organise, and that may mean segmenting, the test cases into separate distinct phases, so that problem solving groups contain the minimum number of participants over three experts.

Another matter for concern for McGraw and Seale is the problem of getting an expert with a lower relative status, but with an important potential contribution, to participate in discussions. The following techniques are designed to overcome that problem and to assist in the management of what is potentially an anarchic situation.

**Group elicitation methods**

McGraw and Seale suggest three methods which are especially suitable for multiple-expert projects. Their approach to **brainstorming** is as follows.

Firstly, explain the rules to all the participants (unfortunately, these are not specified by the authors, which suggests the knowledge engineer may vary the technique according to circumstances). Secondly, give the experts a problem to solve or topic to discuss. The next stage can be achieved in either of two different ways: the experts can either call out their ideas whenever they can be heard, or take turns to contribute. A third variation, not mentioned by McGraw and Seale, is for the knowledge engineer/chairperson (or a highly qualified expert) to call on specific experts after they have made it known that they have a contribution. The knowledge engineer records all the contributions preferably so all the participants can see them. The process is continued until no further contributions are forthcoming or participation is at a fairly low level. The ideas generated by the multi-expert team are discussed by the whole group and form the basis of the agenda for future meetings.

**Consensus decision taking** is a suitable technique to follow the initial brainstorming sessions. The primary aim of this technique is to find the best possible solution. This is achieved by a team of experts voting on a preferred group of solutions or ideas. Voting is by exhaustive ballot and the number of votes required is therefore dependent upon the number of alternatives available for consideration. In their guidelines for consensus decision making McGraw and Seale begin with the knowledge engineer explaining the technique to all the participants and describing the problem they are attempting to solve. The first round of voting takes place with each expert having three votes and with the restriction of only one vote on each option. If after discounting those options which were not supported by anyone the list of alternative solutions is still too large then the team can agree to dispose of some of the options or combine others to reduce the list without voting. Two votes per expert are allowed in the following rounds of voting and this process continues until there is a clear winner or only two options remain. A discussion then takes place with the final one or two options as the subject matter.

**Nominal group technique** is a problem solving procedure which helps reduce conflicts and increase participation. A nominal group is one in which the members are allowed to function independently or even anonymously. The technique begins with an explanation, given by the knowledge engineer, of the procedures to be followed. The participants then list, without discussion, the advantages and disadvantages which they perceive in the problem or the subject under consideration. The knowledge engineer collects all the contributions and compiles a list of all those advantages and disadvantages, combining, altering or clarifying the contributions. Without discussion, the group of experts anonymously rank the items on the list. The knowledge engineer then leads the discussion of the advantages and disadvantages, concentrating upon the priorities the experts used to determine the ranking. After this discussion but without any further discussion the experts list possible solutions to the problem. As with the advantages and disadvantages, the knowledge engineer compiles a list of all solutions to the problem without comment or evaluation and then leads the group discussion to examine the solutions. The aim is simple, to find the best solution. McGraw and Seale admit that more interaction and discussion could take place after the original generation of ideas. The technique is designed to get all to contribute irrespective of their status and to limit counterproductive forms of communication.

**Debriefing** as a multi-expert technique refers quite simply to bringing the session to a close. McGraw and Seale recommend a debriefing session with the whole group followed by debriefing sessions with individual members. They claim that the, 'debriefing process offers knowledge engineers an opportunity not only to obtain consensus from the experts, but also to elicit information concerning each expert's degree of certainty or belief in the information obtained' (p. 22).

The techniques suggested by McGraw and Seale are largely concerned with the problem of getting a group of people to work to together when they may have never worked together before, and/or worked in group problem solving situations before, and/or have little interest in the domains of the others or subject matter under discussion, and achieve an optimum solution. If there is one major error in their reasoning it is this: they assume that because the system demands a combination of expertise from a number of experts the elicitation techniques must be based on a group of experts working as one. It is the role of the knowledge engineer or knowledge engineering team to combine and synthesise the expertise in respect of multiple-expert situations, and synthetic systems in particular. This can be done as well with small groups of experts, two or three, as with large groups, if there is a free flow of information. Group problem solving can arrive at the optimum solution but it can also fail and end up with a compromise which satisfies the members' egos but falls short of the 'best' solution. The old adage that a camel is a horse designed by a committee should be borne in mind. That particular group decision would be a disaster if the goal of the group was to produce an unbeatable showjumper.

Brainstorming in multi-expert situations is no more important than it is in single expert, single domain systems. With many experts the technique can be fashioned to achieve maximum but controlled discussion. This is what makes brain storming sessions so fruitful, the very fact that the discussion brings about comments which would not otherwise have been elicited. One adaptation to the brainstorming session described above would be for each proposer of the suggestion to describe, as objectively and dispassionately as possible, the idea without interruption for five minutes; five minutes is allowed for discussion and clarification and then a vote is taken as to whether the idea should be given further consideration, that is, placed on a short list of possible solutions.

It has always been my understanding that voting on issues or alternatives is not what is meant by consensus and it would appear the authors have misnamed one of their techniques. Consensus is achieved through the power of argument and argument alone, although I have been told that weariness has a lot to do with the final outcome. What the authors are really talking about is the opposite of consensus, in which disagreements are brought to an end by the ballot. This does not lead to a consensus but does get to a solution much quicker.

The advantages and disadvantages of a problem situation may not be applicable to every domain. Indeed it is not clear what is meant by an advantage and how this can then be ranked in terms of priorities. The knowledge engineer should, after discussion with the group, decide what factors are applicable and the listing, ranking and discussion should concern these.

Another problem with this work is the extraordinary mental abilities demanded of the knowledge engineer, who is in the position of leading complex discussions in an area in which at best he is probably a novice and expected to process information such as the list of advantages and disadvantages quickly and creatively. It might be asked, if the knowledge engineer is capable of this, why is he bothering eliciting knowledge which he must already possess (or he would not be able to perform his role during the different techniques)?

Multiple-expert situations and synthetic knowledge-based systems are very difficult projects. There is no clear methodology at this time and there is little in the way of practical commercial experience. It would appear that a balance between group sessions such as those described by McGraw and Seale with individual and very small group sessions accompanied by well presented and freely available (to the team) knowledge engineering documentation is a suitable way to begin such a project, but the knowledge engineer should be aware that constraints in the domain may mean a change in the techniques.

## USING STIMULUS MATERIAL

Case records, plans, drawings and computer printouts make excellent stimulus material for structured interviews. Training videos are another useful resource. The characteristics of the interview are altered by both participants sitting on the same side of the desk studying the same plan or diagram. Sitting on the same side of the desk can be taken as a metaphor for the knowledge engineer's change of status to apprentice. The knowledge engineer and expert work more as a team in the domain than they did as interviewer and respondent. The bias of responses with stimulus material present is heavily orientated towards explanations. It may be applicable to use these stimulus materials as test cases.

## USING THE PROTOTYPE

The prototype and its refinement is one of the most powerful tools for the elicitation of further knowledge. My experience has shown that the first attempt at building a working knowledge-base on any part of the expert's task will be far below optimum performance, as the running of the test cases will show. The reasons for this poor performance are the absence of that knowledge yet to be elicited, inadequate analysis practices and implementation difficulties which have distorted the knowledge. Demonstrating the system and letting the expert use it provides further information which is used to extend the knowledge-base and rectify the errors as well improve the useability of the system.

In using the prototype the expert now takes the role of the user, which implies that the system was built for her use. Irrespective of whether the system was designed for the expert or not, her attempts to use it will provide insights as to the status of the system vis-à-vis useability. To begin with, a demonstration should be given using one of the test cases. Some consistency should be aimed for with the test cases. A test case which serves as an example of the system's capabilities will probably be shown to wider audiences in the future to demonstrate the progress made since the last review. If people can identify with a specific example of the system's functionality then quite complex concepts can be explained within the context of that example. The expert must explore the intricacies of this example test case first of all. Once she has mastered the controls, a more complicated test case is used to refine the knowledge-base. The expert's comments and advice should be carefully noted.

The knowledge engineer should have prepared a bug-list, consisting of deviations from the intended behaviour with reference to the rules, frames or control structure which are thought to be at fault. A fully documented copy of the current knowledge-base should be at hand. The procedure then consists of the knowledge engineer and the expert negotiating between the desired behaviour and how to achieve it. If the expert has become educated in the ways of knowledge engineering then this interaction is easier; otherwise the knowledge engineer should keep his technical jargon to a minimum.

Beware of attempting to adapt the knowledge-base with the expert present. Errors — such as typographical mistakes — reflect badly upon the competence of the knowledge engineer. Waiting for the knowledge-base to be recompiled into object code may frustrate the expert and make her irritable. It is probably better to get the expert's opinions in short bursts and alter the system between meetings.

Depending upon the readability of the knowledge-base language, the amount of comments in the knowledge-base and the proficiency of the expert to understand the knowledge-base, then the knowledge-base itself may be used as a resource to elicit further knowledge and to verify that what has been said has been coded as accurately as possible. Some experts like to be involved to that degree of detail and the extra information they provide or the bugs they discover is highly beneficial to the project; for others, the very idea of reading a knowledge-base is anathema.

## OPTIMISING THE TECHNIQUES

What techniques may be used and when, are important questions for knowledge acquisition. One answer would rely upon the knowledge engineer's increasing abilities twinned with his developing understanding of the particular characteristics of the domain of expertise. However, while accepting that it is the knowledge engineer who is in the front line and must make the decision as to what to use and when, the views of Bainbridge (1986) attempt to answer this question on the merits of the knowledge and the techniques.

The short, but very informative, paper by Bainbridge is a considered comparison of knowledge elicitation techniques. The paper begins with an analysis of the problems which beset the knowledge acquisition phase of an expert systems project and concludes with a number of suggested techniques for different types of knowledge. Readers are advised to study this paper for themselves; however, a brief overview is presented here.

Bainbridge begins by identifying the sources of bias consistent with specific interview situations. These include the cognitive overload of attempting to perform the task and give a running commentary, which has already been mentioned. Secondly, bias may result from the social dimension of elicitation. Elicitation of knowledge is a social act and is therefore constrained by social conventions. It is these social conventions which may introduce bias into the derived information. The expert may be influenced in her responses by what she believes the knowledge engineer wants to hear. Bainbridge also warns of the possible distorting effect of techniques which require the expert to adopt different strategies from the ones she would normally use. The term 'an alien technique' has been used previously in this chapter. It would appear that Bainbridge and myself are referring to the same distorting effects.

Knowledge elicitation techniques, which access knowledge by a different route than those used during the task, generally as an abstraction of the task, may also introduce distortion into the information gathered by these techniques. The veracity of recall without memory aids can never be thoroughly relied upon. A related problem with verbal reporting is the rationalisation of the report when the reporter implies a strict sequence which inevitably introduces inaccuracies into the report. Further rationalisation may also be due to the inadequacy of spoken language and the time constraints of the interview. The difference between the elicitation situation and the task environment may also produce a certain degree of distortion. This is evident in reports of tasks which are performed under time pressure. The report may not represent the reality of the decisions which are reached as the report presumably takes place without those time constraints.

A secondary reason for mentioning Bainbridge's work is so that readers can compare her analysis of knowledge with the speculative analysis of expertise presented in chapter 2 of this book. Bainbridge analyses knowledge into three types. The first is that knowledge which may be represented as structures such as predicates, networks or frames. Secondly, there is knowledge which is based upon memory. Bainbridge adds that this type of expertise can be represented as predicates but is probably not represented that way in the brain. Lastly, there is knowledge which is not represented in the brain in a verbal way.

The first type of knowledge is probably most closely akin to the type of knowledge which would normally be classified as expertise. This consists of knowledge of structures and causal relations, the knowledge of routines and lastly criteria, goals and probabilities. Classes or categories may be represented as hierarchically structured inheritance networks. Each class is described in terms of attribute value pairs and in that respect is very like a frame or object. Knowledge of structures implies a hierarchy of the component parts, and knowledge of causal relationships includes knowledge of constraints upon actions and events. Knowledge of routines includes the deep cognitive skills as well as reasoning strategies, analytical procedures and task operations.

Knowledge as memory falls into two categories. The first is experience and is stored as episodic memory. This is the memory of specific events and specific instances rather than of general classes. The other aspect of memory is the working memory and context memory. This is the space for our calculations and our current opinion of the state of the world, or at least the area we are concerned with. Knowledge which is not represented in the brain in a non-verbal way is deep cognitive knowledge governing motor skills, vision and other automatic or semi-automatic functions.

Whereas the analysis of expertise conducted in chapter 2 was concerned with social content and broad types of mental functioning, Bainbridge has based her analysis on a possible representation in the brain. The study of neurological representational structures is a highly controversial area and is one probably best left out of knowledge engineering (Artificial Intelligence would seem more the place for this sort of speculative enquiry). However, taking the types of knowledge which Bainbridge identifies as semantic categories, her conclusions are insightful and beneficial.

There are two categories of techniques for eliciting knowledge: those that rely on the reports given by an expert (this includes interviews and questionnaire techniques), and those techniques by which knowledge is inferred (this includes observation of the whole or part of the expert's task or a similar task).

Bainbridge concludes that classes, categories and the inheritance hierarchies are best elicited with grouping methods. Interviews are recommended if the type of knowledge to be elicited is mechanisms or descriptions of the structure of hierarchies. For knowledge of causal dynamics (by this I presume she means the task) she recommends interviews, questionnaires and reasoning tasks. Quantitative knowledge which includes criteria is best obtained by using questionnaires with spatial rather than verbal replies for the quantitative dimension. Unfortunately, Bainbridge does not give any further details as to how questionnaires requiring spatial replies might be designed. In respect of strategies and heuristics which support particular expert routines and the goals and sub-goal structure of those routines, verbal protocols and interviews are recommended.

With respect to the knowledge sources related to memory, interviews are suggested for episodic memory; and for the inferences derived from working memory, observation and the analysis of real task decisions including doing the task from memory are recommended. Deep skills are elicited by inferring reasoning processes from observation.

There is undoubtedly more to the efficacy of a technique than the characteristic of the technique itself. Other factors include the personalities of the participants and how they impact upon the acquisition situation with respect to motivation and communication. The proficiency of the knowledge engineer with respect to specific techniques is a direct determinant of the success of the elicitation phase. The management style and management regime of the project have little impact with respect to the methods but are a major determinant of the overall success of the project.

## FIND YOUR OWN (FAVOURITE) TECHNIQUES

No one method is adequate for all knowledge acquisition. Some methods may be applicable to the domain, others may be found to be too difficult. The knowledge engineer must be able to interview without causing himself or the expert any great strain. Once the basic domain knowledge is elicited the later techniques are very much the choice of the knowledge engineer.

There is no substitute for experience. After some time a knowledge engineer develops an insight into which methods are good in respect to specific contexts. With the development of an intellectual appreciation of the techniques comes the development of a particular style and a preference for certain techniques. Lastly, only experience can give the knowledge engineer an appreciation of the constraints imposed by the domain of expertise. The characteristics of the domain play a fundamental part in determining the strategies to use to elicit the domain expertise. And that is the reason why a through knowledge analysis begins with a structured approach to the domain analysis. This is covered in detail in the next chapter.

## SUMMARY

### Overview

- The combination of effective knowledge elicitation methods with a structured approach leads to more effective knowledge acquisition
- Successful knowledge acquisition is achieved by practice until the techniques are mastered
- The techniques of knowledge acquisition and analysis must be used in the context of a general project management structure
- Be expert-led so that you can lead the expert and exercise control over the sessions
- Utilise the opportunities which the different roles offer, from novice to apprentice and finally co-worker
- Look for and react to changes in the role of the expert
- An important role of the orientation phase is to segment the domain into separate phases of investigation

- Discussion of the agenda gives the expert an idea of the knowledge engineer's current understanding and what he hopes to achieve
- Two hours of interviewing without a break is the maximum that should be attempted
- The post-interview discussion gets the expert more involved in the knowledge engineering
- A knowledge-base is a store of detail organised with respect to an overt information processing strategy which is the expert's method

**The techniques**
- THE FOCUSED INTERVIEW is the most like an ordinary conversation. Its purpose is to obtain a broad overview of a topic area. The first focused interviews should be to provide the information for the feasibility study.
- THE STRUCTURED INTERVIEW resembles an interrogation rather than a conversation. Structured interviews are used to gain a deeper insight into the structure of the domain.
- PROBES are used to acquire more information after an initial question has been asked. Types of PROBES:
  —Addition Probe (keep talking about . . . )
  —Reflecting Probe (non-directive instruction to continue)
  —Directive Probe (stop talking about that, say something about this)
  —Change of Mode Probe (keep talking about that but choose a different perspective)
  —Defining Probe (what does that term mean?)
- SELF REPORT AND THINK ALOUD PROTOCOLS are used to elicit detailed information concerning the task and how the expert evaluates progress. This information can be used as the basis of structured interviews.
- REPORT BY COMMENTARY is where the expert explains what is happening or has happened with reference to a documented case study.
- REPERTORY GRIDS are used to elicit the expert's conceptual structure.
- FORWARD SCENARIO SIMULATION assists the knowledge engineer to move from domain analysis to task analysis by getting the expert to talk through a typical problem.
- GOAL DECOMPOSITION also acts as a bridge between domain analysis and knowldge analysis. This time the expert works backward from a solution explaining how it may have come about.
- INQUISITIVE OBSERVATION is where the knowledge engineer interrupts the expert while they are at work and asks for explanations.
- CLASSIFICATION looks at the deep structure of the domain and relationships between the domain objects.
- SYSTEMATIC SYMPTOM-TO-FAULT LINKS investigates the relationship between symptoms, underlying problems and possible solutions.

- DECISION ELICITATION focuses upon the expert's decision making behaviour and the context within which it occurs.
- ANALYTICAL BEHAVIOUR ELICITATION focuses upon the ways in which experts convert and rearrange information.
- REVIEW refers to the interview session in which the knowledge engineer checks his current understanding of the expertise.
- TEACHBACK refers to a change of roles: the knowledge engineer becomes an expert and the expert becomes an examiner.
- THE TRANSLATOR is a person who is not quite an expert and not quite a knowledge engineer but assists in speeding the communication between the expert and the knowledge engineer.
- USE STIMULUS MATERIALS where they are applicable.
- THE PROTOTYPE or latest version of the knowledge-base is the best stimulus material.
- OPTIMISE THE TECHNIQUES by understanding the nature of the expertise which is to be elicited.
- FIND YOUR OWN TECHNIQUES simply refers to becoming more experienced and appreciating the influence of the domain.

**Techniques for dealing with multiple experts**
- BRAINSTORMING gives a group of experts the freedom to experiment with ideas in a group situation.
- CONSENSUS DECISION TAKING involves experts voting on a number of solutions until they find the best.
- NOMINAL GROUP TECHNIQUE keeps the identities of the proposers of ideas secret so that more contributions will be forthcoming.
- DEBRIEFING refers to ending the session.

# 6
## The first interview

**INTRODUCTION**

The first meeting with the expert(s) should not be an interview but a presentation of expert systems technology. If this meeting can be combined with a social occasion then so much the better. However, the major reason for holding this meeting is to introduce the expert(s) to the concepts, procedures and difficulties inherent in knowledge engineering. A presentation should be given by the senior knowledge engineer to the experts covering these main points:

(1) What is an expert system (giving a simplified description)?
(2) Types of expert system (see chapter 1).
(3) What is knowledge and expertise?
(4) Why the expert's particular domain has been identified as one applicable to expert's systems technology.
(5) An overview of knowledge acquisition and elicitation with emphasis upon the problems that might crop up.

**INTERVIEW 1**

There are three major objectives for the first interview between the knowledge engineer and the expert: to characterise the domain, characterise the task and identify and discuss the intended user and environment of the system.

The knowledge engineer cannot be assumed to have any background in the domain. The format of interview 1 is specially designed to achieve a basic knowledge of the domain in the shortest possible time. Interview 1 may not last a single session but must be thought of as a single unit. Interview 1 is different from the focused interviews that follow, as the expert has no role in the criticism of the agenda — that is, no role before the interview begins. The agenda is preset and very largely constructed to provide the answers for a feasibility check list. The major by-product of interview 1 is the requisite knowledge which can be used by the knowledge engineer to begin a structured enquiry.

Before the interview begins, the knowledge engineer explains the purposes of the first interview. This includes making a distinction between the domain and the task. The domain refers to all the objects and concepts specific to the identified area of expertise, the theories and methodologies used to perform the task and a listing of other areas of expertise, world knowledge or common sense that are relevant.

The task refers to what is actually done, the order of sub-tasks and the criteria which discriminate success from failure. The knowledge engineer requires a typology of the tasks performed by the expert, coupled with brief descriptions of each one. The same is true of the solutions. The structure of a typical task, that is, the task(s) adjudged relevant to implementation, should be described interms of a goals and sub-goals structure. If the task can be easily sub-divided into different phases, the nature of, and time taken to accomplish, each phase is important information. Some subjective appreciation of the difficulty of the task and of the various phases is also sought. Peripheral issues include the nature of the planning component, if any, and what administrative functions they perform.

The third issue for interview 1 is the intended environment of the system. This may be different from the expert's current working environment. The feasibility of the system may well rest upon the possibility of adapting computer technology to a hostile physical environment such as an oil rig or a frantic working environment such as a dealing room. This issue and the next two are concerned with the interface between the system and the user.

The fourth issue is the functional mode of the system. The mode of the system not only effects the mode of interaction but is central to defining the main thrust of knowledge engineering. Typical modes for expert systems technology, briefly described in chapter 1, are:

(1) knowledge-based information systems
(2) decision support systems
(3) consultation systems
(4) problem solving systems
(5) coaching systems.

A knowledge-based information system offers the least challenge to the knowledge engineer. An elaborate domain analysis is all that is needed. The task of the system is to interface between a body of static knowledge and a user. The intelligence of the system is manifested far more in the user interface than in the knowledge-base.

A similar application is the decision support system. A detailed decision analysis with emphasis upon the situations in which decisions take place and the information required to make these decisions should suffice. Once again the demonstrative intelligence is in the user interface.

The knowledge acquisition for a consultative system is similar to that needed for the decision support system but includes much more analysis on the reasoning behind the problem solving in the domain. The knowledge engineer must make a greater effort to understand the domain than in the two previous modes. A serious software effort is then required to unite this understanding with the explanation facility in the system.

Problem solving systems or expert simulation systems necessitate the most knowledge engineering. A deep understanding is required of the domain and the task. A lot of effort will be spent tuning up the knowledge-base with expert guided refinements. This is an implementational strategy known as rapid prototyping.

Coaching systems are centred around representing the test cases as scripts. Much of the knowledge acquisition after a brief domain analysis is concerned with the scripting of the test cases.

The analysis of the intended user forms a major part of the knowledge elicitation process. Initial enquiries begin at the first interview with the expert. At this stage a definite decision as to who the intended user is to be may not have been made. The opinions of the expert are important if this is the case. She should be in the best position to know who is and who is not suited to work with the expert system. Some flexibility as to who the intended user will be is preferable but only in as much as the system can address a range of preferred users. The knowledge engineer may consider the source of expertise which may be utilised by a greater number or range of users than the original proposal allowed for. Be warned — the opposite is also true.

The expert herself is the sixth issue for the first interview. Topics such as availability, other roles in the organisation which may conflict with the project, her perceived role in the knowledge engineering and her role in the initiation of the project should be made explicit.

These issues are combined to produce a fairly standard set of questions. The actual format of each question should be adapted to relate more closely to the domain under investigation. Some questions will not apply at all, so the expert should be made aware that 'not applicable' is a valid answer. The knowledge engineer should then probe a little further and find out why.

## QUESTIONS FOR INTERVIEW 1 — THE DOMAIN

1. The project is concerned with a subset of your expertise. Commenting upon this only, would you say that more than one method exists to accomplish your task? How do these methods differ? Which method seems most applicable to expert systems technology and why? Which method is least applicable?
2. Is there more than one theory which applies to the general problem area? Can you explain the differences between the theories?
3. What is the status of the theory (theories)? (e.g. highly specified, derived from empiricism, etc.)
4. What is the role of commonsense knowledge and other knowledge external to the domain?
5. Do other experts in your field agree on all or some of the principles underlying the method(s) you use? What is the nature of the disagreements?
6. Would you say that the domain knowledge is highly structured? or is it unstructured? (this question refers to the categorisational structure of the

concepts and modality of task structure) or would you say your knowledge is fuzzy rather than hard?

7. Are there many concepts in the domain and are these concepts complex or simple?

8. Does the method you use rely upon judgemental behaviour? Would your colleagues make a different judgement in the same circumstances?

9. What formalisms are used to describe the domain and the task?

10. How well is domain knowledge documented? What form does this documentation take? What is the source of this documentation?

11. Is domain knowledge subject to change?

12. Is the domain knowledge reliable? Has it been rigorously tested?


## COMMENTARY ON THE DOMAIN QUESTIONS

*1. The project is concerned with a subset of your expertise. Commenting upon this only, would you say that more than one method exists to accomplish your task? How do these methods differ? Which method seems most applicable to expert systems technology and why? Which method is least applicable?*

If a number of methods are available this could mean there is a choice as to which method the system may use. The reasons why a particular method is chosen by the expert in different circumstances should be explored. The choice of method for the expert system should be the knowledge engineer's responsibility; however, the opinion of the expert is important. The knowledge engineer should not involve the expert in the details of the implementation strategies unless the expert has some background in this area. However, a brief discussion of the options available to the knowledge engineer with respect to implementation may benefit both parties.

*2. Is there more than one theory which applies to the general problem area? Can you explain the differences between the theories?*

A number of competing theories underlying the domain may lead to confusion. The knowledge engineer must ascertain which theories apply to which areas of the domain and what overlap exists. This is not a very major point and should not become the source of a major discussion.

*3. What is the status of the theory (theories)? (e.g. highly specified, derived from empiricism, etc.)*

Following from the previous question, question 3 deals with the complexity of the theories. A knowledge engineering methodology which emphasises the developing understanding of the knowledge engineer must identify any possible bottlenecks to obtaining that understanding. A highly specified theory and in particular one based upon empiricism is preferable. If the theories from which the expertise is derived are low in specificity and founded upon rationalism then the resulting system may be very behavioural.

*4. What is the role of commonsense knowledge and other knowledge external to the domain?*

Any component of the expertise which is based upon commonsense knowledge is potentially problematic. A convenient strategy is to pass the relevant responsibility for this onto the user. Note how already design constraints on the user interface are appearing. Expertise in one domain is always dependent upon some expertise from another domain. Those domains and the relevant overlap must be identified early in the project. The expert is the best person to advise the knowledge engineer if she has sufficient knowledge to assist her understanding in this area and if not where to obtain that understanding. Common types of supporting expertise are statistics, physics and engineering.

*5. Do other experts in your field agree on all or some of the principles underlying the method(s) you use? What is the nature of the disagreements?*

Disagreements between experts will be a problem if the knowledge engineer has to elicit knowledge from more than one expert. This problem is partially solved by managing the disagreements with a comprehensive document structure. It may be possible to use the disagreements and attempt to achieve a consensus among the experts. The technique of multi-expert brainstorming is applicable here. The simplest solution is to identify the 'knowledge Czarina' and take her opinion as being final.

*6. Would you say that the domain knowledge is highly structured? or is it unstructured? (this question refers to the categorisational structure of the concepts and modality of task structure) or would you say your knowledge is fuzzy rather than hard?*

This question is particularly vague as the terms are very subjective. Its main purpose is to initiate a discussion on the broad outlines of the expertise. If the conclusion is that the expertise is highly structured then an approach which elicits knowledge by a divide-and-conquer strategy should be formulated. Expertise which does not break down into easily digestible chunks will mean elicitation and analysis time could well be extended beyond what may be acceptable before there is anything to show for it. Although wrong in principle it is still, nevertheless, better to compromise the knowledge engineer's understanding and implement some part of the system too early than lose the system to management jitters. To avoid this becoming a major managerial confidence issue the demonstrations of the project's progress should be designed with this in mind.

*7. Are there many concepts in the domain and are these concepts complex or simple?*

Complex terms are those which are not in common use such as scientific or mathematical abstractions. If such terms are present, the knowledge engineer must take special care in creating the domain glossary. The knowledge engineer should make a note of the need for some categorisational techniques when the project goes live.

*8. Does the method you use rely upon judgemental behaviour? Would your colleagues make a different judgement in the same circumstances?*

All domains are judgemental to some degree; the question is, to what degree. The types of judgement are also important. Does the expert make decisions based on very subjective interpretations of the facts and do these decisions involve creative solutions? The reader will recall from chapter 2 that creative problem solving is as much, if not more, of a problem as social knowledge.

*9. What formalisms are used to describe the domain and the task?*

A well documented domain of expertise is a precious gift to the knowledge engineer and an unlikely occurrence too. Whatever documentation does exist, the knowledge engineer must be guided by the expert in its use as a resource.

*10. How well is domain knowledge documented? What form does this documentation take? What is the source of this documentation?*

A basis of expertise which undergoes rapid change is a major impediment to the feasibility of the system. For example, a system which assisted experts in the interpretation of company law, assuming such a thing was possible, could well be made obsolete by a chancellor's budget. Who would dare commission such a system to be built? With scientific knowledge, major change is an unpredictable occurrence and therefore quite a reasonable candidate for a knowledge-based system. With poorly specified knowledge the act of knowledge engineering itself may be a factor initiating change. This is not as unlikely as it sounds and the ramifications and potential benefits of this should be explored during the feasibility discussions under the heading of incidental benefits of the project or while discussing this question.

*11. Is domain knowledge subject to change?*

A domain of expertise with unreliable knowledge may well benefit from knowledge engineering in line with the last point. A potential problem with unreliable knowledge is the burden this could well put on the users of the system. They may have to be more expert than the expert system to spot complete garbage being passed as a valid result. Such a situation can only be permitted if the expert system is an assistant to the expert (time saver); otherwise such a system is not feasible for non-expert use.

*12. Is the domain knowledge reliable? Has it been rigorously tested?*

Not all knowledge is testable. Some knowledge just is because the government or some other organisation have decided that is the way it is. If reliability is a major concern then the status of the knowledge may well be important. The question is aimed to identify the degree of uncertainty that the expert recognises in the domain. If reliability is a significant factor and the knowledge is unreliable investigate further and in particular as to how the expert copes with this situation.

## QUESTIONS FOR INTERVIEW 1 THE TASK

1. Are there a number of basic task types? Are there a lot of problem types? How would you categorise these types?
2. Do solutions fall easily into basic categories? How would you categorise them?
3. Is 'no solution' acceptable?
4. Is the 'problem to be solved' aspect of the task well defined or is there a phase of defining the nature of the problem as an initial stage of the whole task?
5. Can the task be broken down to a number of separate stages? Describe each stage as if it was a separate task? What is the interaction between the phases? Which phases are the more difficult and why?
6. How long does it typically take you to perform the whole task? How long does each sub-phase take?
7. What is the form of data you receive?
8. How likely is it that you will question the reliability of the initial data?
9. Does the initial data need interpreting? By whom or what?
10. Could the data be classified as ambiguous or misleading?
11. In what media is the initial problem specified? What media and/or tools are used during the problem solving process?
12. What research is undertaken and from what sources?
13. Is the problem you are solving well constrained?
14. Are there a number of standard routines which are used at any time during the performance of the task?
15. What sort of complications arise during the task?
16. Do problems or errors often occur?
17. Do you sometimes have to backtrack and redo part of the process because of an error or unseen problem?
18. Can you break down the task into the following headings?
(a) problem solving activities
(b) administration
(c) planning
(d) any other (expand).
How much time is spent on each?
19. To what degree is creativity a component of the problem solving activity?
20. Do you call upon the advice or help of any other person during the task?

## COMMENTARY ON THE TASK QUESTIONS

*1. Are there a number of basic task types? Are there a lot of problem types? How would you categorise these types?*

The best situation is the where there are few basic task types. If there are more than a few, and what constitutes more than a few is debatable, then select the most common or those most applicable to expert systems technology for implementation. It is important to restrict the extent of the domain to the choice of the tasks. It is a waste of time to elicit background knowledge for tasks which are not being implemented.

*2. Do solutions fall easily into basic categories? How would you categorise them?*

Single solution types are obviously the best. If there are many types of solutions from the same problem type then there may be user interface problems.

*3. Is 'no solution' acceptable?*

If no solution is an acceptable result, then what are the criteria for aborting the problem solving process? This is a problem within the problem. Complexities may arise if the system is unable to recognise problems without solutions or is too eager in aborting the search for a solution. If this is the case then finding an adequate strategy to come to terms with the no solution case is a priority. The user may recognise garbage as garbage but does not know if the 'I'm sorry that question cannot be answered' reply is genuine. The converse is less of a problem but the possibility of the system pumping out any old rubbish and this not being recognised is cause for concern. The solution is to elicit the checking criteria during the expert's comments on the prototype.

*4. Is the 'problem to be solved' aspect of the task well defined or is there a phase of defining the nature of the problem as an initial stage of the whole task?*

One of the most difficult aspects of an expert's task is the defining or reparameterisation of the initial problem statement. The easiest solution is to pass this task on to the user. If that is not possible then the knowledge engineer must realise that in all likelihood he is building two expert systems in the same domain, one to solve the problem and one to define it. The latter is the more likely to be the cause of the most difficulties.

*5. Can the task be broken down to a number of separate stages? Describe each stage as if it was a separate task. What is the interaction between the phases? Which phases are the more difficult and why?*

If the problem is easily segmented then that bodes well for all the phases of the knowledge engineering. The divide-and-conquer strategy should be utilised at once. Otherwise, some very tricky decisions must be made (under the expert's guidance) and the whole task must be artificially segmented. The result could well be some very unconvincing demonstrations of the developing system.

*6. How long does it typically take you to perform the whole task? How long does each sub-phase take?*

The optimum time for the expert to solve the task is between a half and a full day. If possible this should translate into a system run time of half to one hour. There is no great problem with a task which takes the expert more than one day to complete other than the observation and other task elicitation techniques will probably have to be truncated. The 'Blue Peter' solution (i.e. this is one I made earlier) could come to the rescue if the expert is briefed as to the need of getting the knowledge acquisition session over in one day.

*7. What is the form of data you receive?*

This question is the first of a number which attempt to specify the format of the initial problem. An answer to an earlier question may negate the need to ask a subsequent one. This first question is trying to identify whether the data is machine readable or provided through social contact, or a mix of the two. This will have implications for the user interface.

*8. How likely is it that you will question the reliability of the initial data?*

If the expert questions the reliability of the data what chance has the system? The answer to this question is vital in defining the scope of the system and the responsibilities of the user.

*9. Does the initial data need interpreting? By whom or what?*

Whether the data is reliable or not it may need to be interpreted. If so by whom or what? Is this part of the defining the problem stage of the task or is it a simple process relying on an analytical technique? The knowledge engineer should be clear in his mind as to what happens to the initial problem statement and the concomitant data. Disaster looms if the process of interpretation is subjective or otherwise not amenable to knowledge engineering and the user is incapable of the interpretation stage.

*10. Could the data be classified as ambiguous or misleading?*

Bad data is always a good excuse for a poor result. If this is the expert's excuse for a less than useful result then how can the system fare any better? Is it possible for the system to spot bad data in a way the expert cannot? The power of an expert system in this situation can be increased with the addition of some suitable data processing techniques.

*11. In what media is the initial problem specified? What media and/or tools are used during the problem solving process?*

This question is very similar to question 7 and therefore may have been answered. The point here is the form of the initial enquiry as opposed to the form of the initial data. The likelihood is that the expert system will process a transformation of this initial enquiry; even so, the knowledge engineer requires details of the whole of the domain of expertise.

*12. What research is undertaken and from what sources?*

Research will almost certainly be beyond the scope of the expert system so any research the expert does will have to be performed by the user. The system may assist the user with research by suggesting likely sources of information but if this is beyond the user then the feasibility of the system is in doubt.

*13. Is the problem you are solving well constrained?*

It is difficult to see how the answer to this can be anything other than subjective. Well constrained compared with what? Any question may initiate a debate between the knowledge engineer and the expert, this one is no exception. The aim of the question is to discover how the task or problem statement develops throughout the solving process.If the problem space, which is defined by the number of possible solutions or transformations at any one time, is very large then the problem is poorly constrained and this implies some great difficulties will arise during the elicitation of the task structure.

*14. Are there a number of standard routines which are used at any time during the performance of the task?*

Standard routines are the bread and butter of the computer programmer and the knowledge engineer alike. If the expert's task contains many of these routines then implementation is made simpler. The knowledge engineer should attempt to gauge the complexity of these routines as the elicitation of them may be a problem even if implementation is not. Assuming that elicitation does not seem to be a potential problem then the knowledge engineer can plan for an early implementation as soon as the domain analysis is complete and the task analysis has settled down. An early implementation is not a good idea if the orientation to the domain is not fully completed. However, the boost a working prototype gives to the project team is considerable. The temptation to rush ahead and get something running is irresistible, but it should be remembered the success of the project is decided when the work has been done not before most of it has been started. Do not rush towards a working prototype if it means the understanding of the knowledge engineer is likely to suffer.

*15. What sort of complications arise during the task?*

As handling complications is what distinguishes the expert from the novice then this is a very important question. If there are many complications and the strategies for dealing with these are not handled with initiative then the feasibility of the project suffers.Further investigation is required until the knowledge engineer is satisfied that the elicitation and implementation of these strategies is possible before the project should be given the go-ahead. Not all the solutions to all the problems can be known in advance of the feasibility study but the knowledge engineer should be confident that there are no potential problems which will wreck the project.

*16. Do problems or errors often occur?*

An expertise which is prone to errors or complications will cause great problems to the knowledge engineer.There is an added dimension of spotting the errors and correcting them. As with the previous question (which impinges upon this one) the knowledge engineer must investigate this area before making claims about the feasibility of the project.

17. *Do you sometimes have to backtrack and redo part of the process because of an error or unseen problem?*

Backtracking and redoing is what expert systems are good at and thus form a major plus for feasibility as information processing strategies are very bad at this.

18. *Can you break down the task into the following headings:*
*(a) problem solving activities*
*(b) administration*
*(c) planning*
*(d) any other (expand).*
*How much time is spent on each?*

Looking at the expert's task from the wider perspective and comparing this with the preconceived ideas of the role of the system is very illuminating. It may be possible to combine some of the administrative tasks which the expert performs in conjunction with the main problem solving task without a great deal of extra work. Conversely, an administrative task may be vital to the prospective expert system task and not realised.

19. *To what degree is creativity a component of the problem solving activity?*

Creative solutions are more than a problem — they are a no-go area for expert systems technology.

20. *Do you call upon the advice or help of any other person during the task?*

The expert may discuss her current task with others for social rather than occupational reasons. In that case her confidant is not telling her anything that she could not have thought of herself. If, however, the expert calls on the advice of others because they provide information which is beyond her then this does not not bode well for the system.

**QUESTIONS FOR INTERVIEW 1 — THE ENVIRONMENT**

1. Are there any environmental constraints which either apply to the performance of the task or may impinge on situating the final system?
2. Can you describe the environment in terms of illumination, noise levels and any other physical constraints?
3. Is there a large amount of movement in the environment which may hinder interaction with the system via a computer terminal?
4. Is the perceived environment of an industrial nature?
5. Does the system have to be distributed amongst a number of simultaneous users?
6. What other systems have to be interfaced with the proposed expert system? What is your interaction with these systems at the current time?
7. Is the environment supplying data directly to the expert system?
8. What environmental changes are likely to follow the introduction of the expert system?

## COMMENTARY ON ENVIRONMENT QUESTIONS

Most of these questions are quite straightforward and do not need any explanation. It is unlikely that all the questions need to be asked as the expert will probably give most of the required information concerning the environment after one question. In that case the questions act as a checklist. To assist the knowledge engineer I have expanded the topics covered somewhat implicitly in these eight questions into a check list in Fig. 6.1. If

Time constraints (real time)
Control or interface to important/dangerous machinery
Interface to automatic system
Human perception practicalities
Human input practicalities
Special equipment needed
Special terminals
Hand-held equipment
Voice-operated equipment
Single-input situation
Multi-input situation
Passive user
User as problem maker

Fig. 6.1 — Checklist for topics concerning the environment.

there are some problems with the environment the knowledge engineer should consult an experienced hardware specialist.

## QUESTIONS FOR INTERVIEW 1 — MODALITY

1. Which one of the following modes do you consider your expertise is most applicable to: knowledge-based information systems, decision support systems, consultation systems, problem solving systems, coaching systems?

## COMMENTARY ON MODALITY

Up to this point the knowledge engineer may already have a strong feeling as to what the prospective mode of the system will be. It is probable that management believe that they are commissioning a specific type of expert system. The expert too will have some views on the mode of simulation which is possible or will benefit her. There should be no problem with this question if they understand the differences between the terms.

## QUESTIONS FOR INTERVIEW 1 — THE USER

1. What does the client understand of your expertise?
2. What is the nature of your interaction with your client.

3. Describe who in your view is the typical user.
4. Do you envisage a spread of users? What distinguishes these users from each other?
5. Will the users expect thesystem to provide them with explanations of the reasoning process?
6. Will the users wish to use the system as a coaching system to raise their level of expertise?
7. How much interaction will a user need with the system?
8. Will a well structured help system be an important feature?
9. Do some of your clients perform some of the expert task themselves?

## COMMENTARY ON USER QUESTIONS

It may not always be clear who the user will be at the early stages of the project. Quite often it is a function of the feasibility study to identify the potential user of the system. In any case it should be the function of the feasibility study to verify the assumptions made about the potential user and perhaps make suggestions concerning the scope of the users.

*1. What does the client understand of your expertise?*

Expert systems should provide on-line help or documentation as a matter of course. The less the user knows about the expertise the more elaborate those peripheral features have to be. The style of the explanation features are also dependent upon the user's level of knowledge. The knowledge engineer must build a system which is tailored to the user and reflects the current working methods of the expert.

Users with a high degree of knowledge are as much a cause of problems for the knowledge engineer and system designer as users with little or no knowledge of the expertise. The explanation facilities will have to be very detailed and the system will be expected to have a high degree of reliability.

*2. What is the nature of your interaction with your client?*

The expert may perform a social role with respect to the client, such as reassuring her that their problem is in good hands or discussing the result or problems in a intelligible manner. This will be beyond the expert system. The question raises the issue as to what extent the expertise can be separated from the expert.

*3. Describe who in your view is the typical user?*

The expert's view of the user should be noted carefully and compared with an actual identified user.

*4. Do you envisage a spread of users? What distinguishes these users from each other?*

A spread of users in terms of their understanding of the expertise, general intelligence levels and status within the company can cause great problems to the designers of the system. A target user must be defined, either the most numerous, most important or most needful, noting that these categories are not mutually exclusive. The system is then designed with this person in mind. Adaptations can then be made to make the system available to other target groups.

5. *Will the users expect the system to provide them with explanations of the reasoning process?*

If users don't want explanations then the explanative power of the system can be restricted to what the development team require for debugging purposes. If they do, the expert is a reasonable source as to what level these explanation should be pitched.

6. *Will the users wish to use the system as a coaching system to raise their level of expertise?*

Help text should be the responsibility of the expert or assistant to the expert. As an aside, a well written help text can be a good knowledge acquisition resource.

7. *How much interaction will a user need with the system?*

The amount of interaction with the system is a critical factor. The code which represents the interface capabilities of an expert system is usually over half of all the code. If there is to be a large amount of varied interaction then the computational cost of processing this information even before the knowledge-base is considered may be prohibitive. Although conventional software is less expensive to construct on a line-for-line basis than expert systems software a lot of conventional software will be expensive.

8. *Will a well structured help system be an important feature?*

The answer to this question may have already been given; its inclusion here acts as a reminder.

9. *Do some of your clients perform some of the expert task themselves?*

If the clients and by implication potential users of the system do some of the task already then this is a great boost to the feasibility of the system. It may be that the prototypes can take over this area and extend it. The benefits would be the system being more easily accepted by the user and saving time and money at an earlier date.

**THE EXPERT**

1. What is your current availability to participate in knowledge elicitation sessions? How is that likely to change in the coming months?
2. What is your reason for participating in this project?
3. What contribution other than providing knowledge do you think you can make?
4. What other roles do you have in the organisation? Can you see any reason why these roles might conflict with the development of the expert system?
5. Are you still learning?

6. Do training procedures exist for people to take over some of your tasks or to become expert themselves?
7. Do you think you will have any problems in explaining what you do?

## COMMENTARY ON EXPERT QUESTIONS

*1. What is your current availability to participate in knowledge elicitation sessions? How is that likely to change in the coming months?*

This is the crunch question. Without a readily available expert there is no expert system project.

*2. What is your reason for participating in this project?*

Why the expert is participating is an obvious determinant to her degree of participation or non-participation, which is important once the initial enthusiasm has worn off.

*3. What contribution other than providing knowledge do you think you can make?*

The expert does not have to contribute anything other than knowledge. However, it is possible the expert may have a managerial role within the project or be the author of the help text. Depending upon her enthusiasm for the project she may be an important ally in any battles to come.

*4. What other roles do you have in the organisation? Can you see any reason why these roles might conflict with the development of the expert system?*

It is important to know what other roles the expert has in the organisation as they may conflict with the project, either by reducing the time available for elicitation or where a role elsewhere in the company which the expert values is threatened by the implications of the introduction of the expert system or the expert system technology.

*5. Are you still learning?*

While it may be argued that we never really stop learning different aspects about our jobs, it may be a problem if it is likely that fundamental changes in the expert's way of doing things follow some event. Any domain of expertise which is continually teaching the expert something suggests that there is a strong element of creativity involved.

*6. Do training procedures exist for people to take over some of your tasks or to become expert themselves?*

There are two reasons for asking this question. The first is concerns the feasibility of the project. If there are training procedures and the flow of expertise from person to person is good then it may be difficult to convince senior management that an alternative computational system is required along with the human experts. The enthusiasm for the project may well be half hearted if she knows that there is an adequate supply of humans to do the job in the future. Secondly excepting the previous point, training procedures can form a valuable resource for the knowledge engineer. They can be used as the subject matter for discussion, directly to increase the knowledge engineer's own knowledge and incorporated as part of the help text in the final system.

*7. Do you think you will have any problems in explaining what you do?*
There will be problems with the expert's powers of explanation. This question should lead to a discussion of these potential and probably inevitable problems.

There is probably far too much information required from interview 1 to be gathered at one meeting. The knowledge engineer may be lucky to fit all of his questions in two sessions of about two to three hours each. Whatever time is taken, this information should provide the bulk of the feasibility report and the extra information can be used to plan the entire acquisition part of the project and form the basis of the first interviews in the first cut phase. Another important result of the orientation phase is the good working relationship between the participants.

## SUMMARY

- The very first meeting (meeting 0) between the knowledge engineer and expert should include a presentation of knowledge engineering techniques and concepts
- The major objectives or interview 1 are: to characterise the domain, characterise the task and identify the intended user
- Interview 1 may take more than one session but should be thought of as a single unit
- The major by-product of interview 1 is the extra information which is used as the basis of a structured enquiry when the knowledge acquisition phase truly begins
- The difference between the domain and the expert's task should be made explicit
- The major topics for interview 1 are: the domain of expertise, the expert's task, the intended environment, the functional mode, the user and finally the expert

# 7
# Planning and preparation

**INTRODUCTION**

All phases of an expert system project must be planned. This chapter is concerned with the planning and preparing for the interviews that is the basic organisation needed to accomplish successful interviews, gain a good understanding of the domain and construct a useful document set. Chapter 10 deals with the wider aspect of project planning and how that relates to knowledge elicitation.

There are two types of analysis. The first type refers to the assimilation of the recording of the interview and any artifacts generated. The second type of analysis refers to taking the product of the previous form of analysis and the knowledge engineer's general understanding of the domain and constructing an intermediate representation or organisation from which a knowledge-base is written.

Preparation also has two meanings. The first is the all-encompassing preparation for the task of eliciting knowledge in an unknown domain. Sadly, too few knowledge engineers are prepared for knowledge elicitation and come to grief without a clear understanding of why. The second meaning of preparation refers to the tasks which are undertaken to ensure the success of the interview.

If a knowledge engineer is following the methodology laid out here, then he will have an overall appreciation of the difficulty of the task which awaits him, and will have availed himself of the questionnaires suitably customised to the domain in question. It is to be hoped an appreciation of the difficulty of the knowledge elicitation task is also shared by the prospective expert and more importantly by the management team.

**THE INITIAL PLAN**

The knowledge engineer who attempts to plan the whole of the knowledge elicitation phase is in a very difficult situation. There is little comfort in the fact that he is not the only one who is unaware of the problems that lie ahead. This, coupled with the obligatory optimism with expert systems projects, means time scales tend to be hopelessly too short. More realistic time scales result from appreciating the knowledge engineering phase as a major part of the whole project.

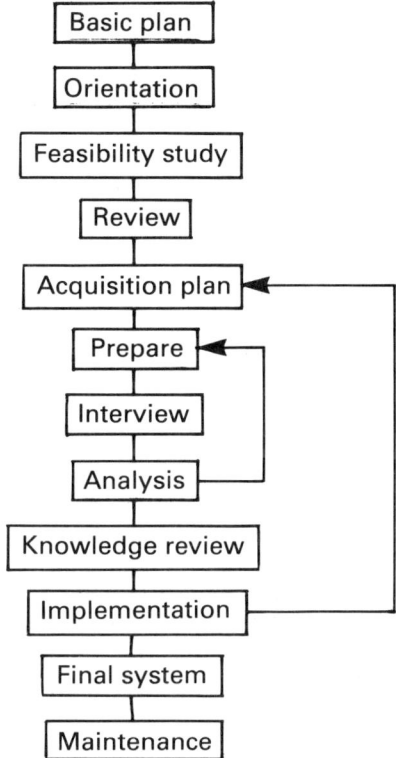

Fig. 7.1 — The phases of an expert system project.

Knowledge elicitation divides into eight major areas. They are the basic plan and primary preparation, the orientation phase, the feasibility study, the major plan and second orientation, prototype elicitation, main phase elicitation, refinement and tuning and lastly maintenance.

The basic plan is concerned with the knowledge engineer's initial reactions to the project. There are three concerns at this time: preparing for and arranging meetings with the expert, the client and prospective user of the system; holding those meetings; and writing the feasibility report on the basis of the information gathered. The initial meeting, rather than the first interview, is more an exchange of ideas and expectations than a search for information. However, much useful information may stem from it about the domain and the project including the participants in it.

The reader may adapt the draft questionnaires for the succeeding meetings with the expert, client's management, and prospective users. By using and adapting the format of interview 1 which was presented in the previous chapter the knowledge engineer can be assured that he has asked the pertinent questions. How these questions are followed up in whatever time is available is very much a matter for the knowledge engineer.

An important part of the orientation process, but one which is often neglected, is the elicitation of the prospective users of the system. The basic plan should take account of the importance of this process and allot some time for a meeting with one of the prospective users. This may mean spending some time to identify who this person will be. The meetings with the client's management, who are probably responsible for commissioning the feasibility study, may take place before the knowledge engineer has met the expert. If this is so, it is important to discuss the initial conclusions of the first interview with the expert at a later date with the client's management.

When all the meetings have been held and the analysis is complete the feasibility report must be written. The general opinion is that it is a very poor feasibility report which does not support the conclusion that an expert systems approach is justified. However, the knowledge engineer should weigh the consequences of an over enthusiastic report very carefully, after all, it is the knowledge engineer who will be responsible for the analysis and elicitation of the knowledge. If this is not the case and another person will provide most of the knowledge engineering, then the first problem in the project is exposed. The individual that does the research and writing of the feasibility report should be the knowledge engineer who is responsible for eliciting the knowledge. If he has any reservations as to the applicability of the expertise to an expert systems approach then he should make those reservations clearly and positively — suggesting strategies which may solve the problems. An expert systems approach may be technically feasible with reservations but infeasible in cost terms. More will be said of these issues in chapter 9.

Assuming that the feasibility of the project is accepted, the first task of the knowledge engineer is to construct a plan of the knowledge acquisition phase which corresponds with the project plan. The development of these two plans should run concurrently. The knowledge engineer produces the knowledge *acquisition* plan largely on his own, but with guidance from the expert, and this has a sizeable input to the project plan.

A precursor to any planning is to refresh the memory as to the fine details of the project, and in particular those factors which were not made explicit in the feasibility study. This may mean listening to the tapes again or just reading the analyses of the interviews. It is here the knowledge engineer attempts to establish the work needed to accomplish a working prototype knowledge-base and the number of cycles required to complete the knowledge analysis for the whole system. Both of these concerns rely upon a rational segmentation of the task. The interviews carried out for the feasibility study should contain the requisite information for this planning stage. If they do not — because the clients have changed their requirements — then an interview should be arranged to obtain the information as a priority.

The knowledge acquisition plan should be detailed enough to structure the project on a day-by-day basis and flexible enough to be modified without causing great delays. The plan should detail the areas of knowledge which are to be elicited, when this will take place, and by what methods. Time should be allotted for acquiring proficiency in using a shell or knowledge representation language as well as for reviewing and ordering the information which is gained. Time to elicit feedback from the prospective users of the system should be budgeted as well as administrative tasks concerning the project.

Acting upon the plan, the knowledge engineer begins the second and major orientation into the domain. This could begin with a discussion of the feasibility study and knowledge acquisition plan with the expert with reference to how the expert sees the acquisition phase progressing. The knowledge engineer may have been over-enthusiastic with some of the time scales and the sooner this is identified the easier changes to the plan can be made. If the knowledge engineer is to be expert-led then the knowledge elicitation plan must be the result of mutual effort. A brainstorming session is another way of beginning the knowledge engineering phase and is covered elsewhere.

The orientation should continue with a recap of the domain analysis as perceived by the expert. Preparation of a domain analysis document which has been sent to the expert in advance of the first meeting after the acceptance of the feasibility study is the preferred way of checking the knowledge engineer's understanding. A review interview (see previous chapter) is another way of organising this session.

As a result of the second orientation and feasibility review, the expert obtains a clearer picture of the knowledge engineer's current state of understanding, his objectives and how he intends to achieve them. If the knowledge engineer who performed the feasibility study is not continuing with the project then his replacement must begin as if he was performing the analysis for a feasibility study: that is, he must begin with interview 1 and build up his own domain analysis document, review this with the expert and plan the project accordingly. An attempt to use the previous knowledge engineer's work will result in failure, sooner rather than later unless the priority is to understand the domain. A good knowledge foundation is essential, even if this means repeating much of the initial work.

The rolling analysis which takes place interview by interview is facilitated by, and largely concerned with, a document set. These documents may exist as lists, glossaries, textual forms or diagrams, and are the data used for the deeper analysis needed to construct a knowledge-base. Each domain demands a slightly different collection of documents but principal members are:

Glossary of main terms
List of indisputable facts
Project log
Rational task description
Primitives inventory
Task analysis diagrams
Derived knowledge book
Interview transcripts

Test-case analyses
Decision analysis book
Analytical techniques analysis book.

## GLOSSARY

The Glossary is one of the most important documents in the beginning of the project. With so many new terms, meanings and concepts to be learned there must be a systematic method for storing and accessing these terms. As the project progresses this document is used less and less but should always feature as part of the knowledge engineer's personal review as some terms will inevitably slip away when not in regular use.

## FACTS BOOK

Every domain has a number of facts which are undisputed and always true. The temperatures at which metals melt, the electrical power used by a particular component are examples of indisputable facts.

## RATIONAL TASK DESCRIPTION

The document describing the rational task description is derived from the elicitation sessions using such techniques as think-aloud protocols, forward scenario simulation or goal decomposition. This description of the task is simplistic in that it avoids any problems and likely complications. This then becomes the model for the first attempt at implementation.

## PRIMITIVES INVENTORY

This document lists the primitive operations as induced by the knowledge engineer. It is very likely to be the result of a detailed task analysis. Each primitive should be documented with the inputs and outputs if that is applicable and a structured English or pseudo-code definition. The document acts as a reference source when checking on the completeness of the system.

## INTERVIEW TRANSCRIPTS BOOK

If the interviews are fully transcribed, which is preferable but not necessary, then this book represents the depository, along with the agendas and preparation for the relevant interviews. The use of a word processor allows a second edited version of the transcript to be created containing the more important information derived from the interviews. Without full transcription it is more efficient to paraphrase and selectively transcribe the significant utterances. This is stored in the interview transcripts book. At suitable times this book should be indexed and a contents page created making it easier to find the relevant topics when needed.

## TEST CASE ANALYSIS BOOK

The test cases are a special type of interview transcript. They represent the first standards by which success is evaluated. The test case analysis book details the expert's explanations as to how she performed the test case, but most importantly it also details the reasoning strategies which it is believed lie behind the expert's performance. The result is a mixture of formalisms: the transcript, the knowledge engineer's analysis of the reasoning strategies and a task description, more complex than the rational task description, which adequately describes the test case. This document may be supplemented with printouts of the system's attempts to duplicate the expert's behaviour andthe expert's comments upon the system's performance.

## DERIVED KNOWLEDGE BOOK

During the knowledge elicitation phases the knowledge engineer will wish to check a number of facts, opinions and expectations with the expert. This is the technique known as review. The derived knowledge book is the collection of these numbered propositions which make up the subject matter of the review sessions along with the expert's comments and corrections. A contents page or index should be compiled and updated at periodic reviews of this information.

## DECISION ANALYSIS BOOK

This is the record of the decisions taken by the expert in line with the decision analysis technique detailed in the last chapter. The document should contain a detailed description of the situation when the decision is taken, what choices are available, the determinants of the choices and what direct and indirect changes follow from a particular decision.

## ANALYTICAL TECHNIQUES ANALYSIS BOOK

As with the decision analysis book, the analytical techniques analysis book describes the processes of changes in representations which the expert carries out during the performance of the task.

## KNOWLEDGE ACQUISITION PLAN

This document lists the aims and aspirations of the knowledge engineer in terms of specific goals and milestones, ensures that interviews are thought out well in advance, and changes justified in terms of what is currently planned. The knowledge acquisition plan is the central management tool for the knowledge engineer. Its regime is not binding but provides a basis on which the knowledge engineer can satisfy himself that his actual behaviour is achieving the goals set out in the plan. The knowledge acquisition plan is a personal document: it should not become part of the project management's tool kit as this will reduce the flexibility which the knowledge engineer has carefully included.

## THE PROJECT LOG

The project log, like the knowledge elicitation plan, is the private resource of the knowledge engineer. The knowledge engineer should document his ignorance and how it was overcome (or why not), what difficulties were experienced, what was done, when and why, and the consequences of previous actions, the first drafts of vague future plans and most importantly the lessons learnt.

### Interview analysis

Knowledge elicitation is a very repetitive business. The knowledge engineer holds an interview, analyses an interview, plans and prepares for an interview and holds another interview. The dynamics within the interview change, the roles of the participants change and the techniques used change but the analysis, planning and preparation hardly vary at all.

## WITH TRANSCRIPTION

Getting someone else (i.e. an audio typist) to transcribe the interviews is the easiest and least time consuming method. In the author's experience it is unlikely that a typist will be found who is prepared to devote the three hours, or so, needed to transcribe one hour of tape. It is a terrible job which most typists will avoid if they can. Their task may be made easier if the knowledge engineer provides them with a list of technical terms that are likely to feature in the recording and with which they will have trouble. Unless the transcript can be provided quickly there is little reason in having the tape transcribed at all.

It is up to the knowledge engineer whether he listens to the tape or just reads the transcript. Reading the transcript is faster. Information can be selectively highlighted. As the knowledge engineer performs this process he should be preparing a list of further questions to be asked at the next or future interviews. The information derived from the transcript can then be posted to the relevant documents.

## WITHOUT TRANSCRIPTION

The procedures for analysis, planning and preparation are as follows. The knowledge engineer listens to the audio tape (or watches the video recording if he is so lucky) and takes only the briefest of notes, mainly to remind him as to the position on the tape where a topic begins. This first replay of the interview is to refresh the memory as to exactly what happened. The knowledge engineer then replays the tape for a second time. This time he concentrates upon those topics judged important, simultaneously noting all the definitions for appending to the glossary and all no-nonsense facts for the indisputable facts book.

A useful format for selective transcriptions of important parts of the tape is a copy of the agenda or questionnaire. The expert's words, or paraphrases thereof, are word-processed into the relevant places. This technique reveals any obvious mismatches between the objectives set by the question and the replies as they are now understood. This is demonstrated to a greater degree if the knowledge engineer had time to carry out a second pass at preparation (see below) and uses a copy of that particular file as a basis of the analysis file. After completing this transcription stage it is unlikely that the knowledge engineer will listen to the tape again. However, the tape should be filed away, and its contents, date, participants and computer text files recorded in the log.

This transcribing process is central to the developing understanding of the knowledge engineer. Quite a few separate tasks may be combined. Apart from updating the glossary and facts book the knowledge engineer can prepare for subsequent interviews — the next one in detail, later ones as collections of topics to be covered. The compilation of a list of propositions for review can also be extended.

When the interview has been heard for the second time, and the documentation completed, the interview as a whole should be assessed from the point of view of the objectives set down in the project log. The objectives fall into three categories, technical, managerial and personal. Technical issues include whether the knowledge engineer had the requisite amount of knowledge to hold the interview, if the method chosen was the right one, why the expert had trouble with a particular topic, and overall whether the interview was a success with reference to the analysis.

Managerial issues are largely concerned with time. What time has been used up so far in this area, how long is left to elicit the rest of the information and what is the current estimate for completing this area of the domain or task? Is there a requirement for more (human or other) resources? Are there any problems others should be made aware of? The knowledge engineer must assess if any aspect of the last meeting means a change in the knowledge elicitation plan or has any implications for implementation.

The personal issues concern the participants and their subjective opinions of the project. Very largely these will be the opinions of the knowledge engineer. However, a very communicative and involved expert may confide in the knowledge engineer at the end of the interview.

A detailed report of the interview under those three headings provides the knowledge engineer with an aide-mémoire that is helpful in passing on experiences to others and as a source for making decisions and writing reports.

**PLANNING FOR ACQUISITION**

The knowledge engineering plan — possibly kept as part of the log — is the repository of ideas concerning future interviews deposited either during the analysis of the interviews or when the idea materialised. Constant reference to the log, or even better a good indexing system should mean that details will not be forgotten. The plan should be fairly specific as to what areas of the domain or task are to be covered, when, and by what method. This should largely be a list of topics which make up those areas of knowledge which must be elicited before an implementation goal can be achieved. As the knowledge engineer accomplishes the elicitation of each topic, the details of the duration in time, number of interviews and amount of analysis and any problems are documented. The knowledge engineer probably does not spend as much time building expert systems as he does writing reports — it just seems that way — having information for the reports at his fingertips can't be a mistake. The information collected often feeds back into the project management structure assisting the planning of later parts of the project.

The knowledge acquisition plan coupled with the log is the knowledge engineer's most authoritative record of the current state of the project and of the decisions which have been taken. One of the most important decisions is when to close the knowledge acquisition process and concentrate upon implementation and refinement. This is one of the most difficult and important decisions which will be taken during the project. As will be seen in the next chapter, expert systems projects are somewhat open ended when it comes to knowledge acquisition. Terminate the knowledge acquisition phase too early and the implementation phase suffers through lack of completeness, and refinement becomes confused with the elicitation of fresh knowledge.

Planning the next interview should preferably be taken in two phases. The first phase is to edit the document which has been built up during the analysis of the previous interview and which is intended to represent the main thrust of the subsequent interview. The first step in this edit is to state clearly and explicitly the purposes of the interview. If there is any problem in doing this it suggests a weakness in the planning for this stage of the knowledge acquisition. The knowledge engineer must consider the plan of the knowledge elicitation phase, ask whether there is a stage missed out which is therefore causing the difficulties in specifying the objects of the next interview. Or perhaps some event has occurred which now makes this next interview superfluous and this requires a change to the plan. The knowledge engineer may be attempting to elicit an area of knowledge which should be left until other topics have been covered — the plan has the topics incorrectly scheduled. Whatever the reason the knowledge engineer must be able to find a simple, concise statement which represents the purpose of the interview.

After stating the purposes of the interview, expanded into the first paragraph, the next step is to create the agenda. The actual format of this is left to the individual tastes of the knowledge engineer. However, one method would be to draw up a number of introductory questions in separate sections with easiest questions and easiest section to the forefront. The first section should deal with clearing up details from the previous interview, including those points which are pending from the interview because the expert was unsure of her answer and promised to research the details or problems which emerged. This first section may include queries caused by a word or two that cannot be distinguished from the tape, and which the knowledge engineer, quite correctly, refuses to guess. The completion of other sections of the agenda may require the knowledge engineer to refer back to the analysis of earlier interviews. Where a topic area looks too broad for a number of concise questions, derive some questions to explore the topic in preparation for delimiting the area for a later interview.

## SECOND LEVEL PREPARATION

After the knowledge engineer has constructed the agenda/plan/sample questions for the next session he should take sometime to review the agenda on a separate sheet of paper or copy of the file. The expert should not have access to this, as it is more likely to confuse than enlighten. The main function of second level preparation is to look for problems in the first level preparation; this is done by the knowledge engineer putting himself in the role of the expert. Taking this role is only possible if the knowledge engineer has a good idea of the sort of objections the expert might raise to the line of questioning. The knowledge engineer asks himself if he is using concepts with which the expert will be unfamiliar and tries to imagine what kind of answers he will get and the possible issues which will be raised. The goal is to be so well prepared that questions should only rarely be misunderstood. If they are, a second line of defence exists in terms of some brief notes describing what each question means. This will give the expert confidence in the knowledge engineer's ability and assist with the flow of the interview.

## SUMMARY

- There are two types of analysis: the assimilation of interview material and intellectual effort required before implementation
- There are two types of preparation: preparing oneself for the task of eliciting knowledge and the preparation required for an interview
- There are eight major areas of knowledge elicitation: primary preparation, the orientation phase, the feasibility study, the major plan, prototype elicitation, main phase elicitation, refinement and lastly maintenance
- The basic plan should take into account meetings with prospective users and any management personnel who are involved
- The knowledge engineer should be the author of the feasibility study
- Make sure the knowledge acquisition plan corresponds with the project plan
- Before writing the knowledge acquisition plan, refresh the memory as to the details of the project
- The knowledge acquisition plan should be detailed enough to structure

the project on a daily basis but flexible enough to be modified without causing delays
- The use of other knowledge engineers' analysis will probably result in failure
- Typists hate transcribing interviews
- Listen to the interview recording twice
- Selective transcribing may be carried out by the knowledge engineer while simultaneously updating the document set and preparing for the next interview
- The objectives of the interview fall into three categories: technical, managerial and personal
- The project log is for the knowledge engineer's subject appreciation of the project
- After preparing an interview try to look at the content from the expert's point of view

## THE DOCUMENT SET

— Glossary of main terms
— List of indisputable facts
— Project log
— Rational task description,
— Primitives inventory
— Task analysis diagrams
— Derived knowledge book
— Interview transcripts
— Test case analyses
— Decision analysis book
— Analytical techniques analysis book
— The log

# 8

# Knowledge analysis

**INTRODUCTION**

The cycle of preparation/interview/analysis is broken only by a major analysis. A major analysis is performed if the investigation into the sub-domain is considered to be complete, preferably by both the knowledge engineer and the expert. Alternatively, there may be a pressing requirement for a new version of the system. If the latter is the case, then the running system should be used as a resource in completing the investigation of the specific sub-domain. There is always a pressure to move on to the deeper investigation of more of the domain, so if a major analysis is called for before the analysis is complete the knowledge engineer must, as a priority, document the incompleteness. Plans to complete the acquisition of an incomplete area of knowledge should be stored away in the knowledge acquisition plan. It is very likely they will be needed.

The format of the knowledge analysis is called an intermediate representation. The intermediate representation should adequately represent the knowledge in a way which eases the transition to the knowledge representation language or other computer language. There are many choices of intermediate representation available to the knowledge engineer. Only a subset will be reviewed here. More important than the choice of intermediate representation are the reasons for choosing it. One of the factors involved in that decision is the requirements of the system implementer. The task of implementation may be performed entirely by the knowledge engineer responsible for eliciting the knowledge, shared with another knowledge engineer or given over entirely to someone else. Whoever does build the knowledge-base he should be familiar with the knowledge analysis and have the working knowledge of the task. The source of meta-knowledge (i.e. knowledge about the expertise) comes from the knowledge engineer and the artifacts of the acquisition process, primarily the knowledge engineering documentation set. The system implementer may have a preference for a particular type of intermediate representation from his acquaintance with the knowledge analysis or his own programming background. If so, that preference is an obvious candidate for the intermediate representation. All that is required before the first major analysis is verification that these previous discussions concluded with the right decision. In the area of domain expertise the knowledge engineer must be guided by the expert. In the area of implementation he is guided by the implementer.

In the situation where no preference has been indicated or the knowledge engineer responsible for acquisition is also responsible for implementation then other factors must be considered. One factor is the degree of analysis which has been performed and corresponding understanding in the area to be implemented. If there is a high degree of understanding then only a small amount of intermediate representation will be needed for efficient implementation. Correspondingly, there is no requirement for a particularly complex representation. In essence the documentation set coupled with the knowledge engineer's own limited but vital expertise makes the step from analysis to implementation a much less traumatic one than would be the case if the knowledge acquisition phase was not oriented towards understanding.

Another factor is the complexity and representative power of the knowledge representation language, shell or computer programming language. A high degree of representative power in the implementation medium requires only a sketch of the structure of the task. The knowledge representation language itself, devoid of peripheral complications, is the ideal intermediate representation. Structured diagrams, flow charts, task analysis trees, data-flow diagrams or augmented transition networks and other graphical representations act as a sketch of the implementation space. The intermediate representation is only a guide — the specificity of the domain knowledge is held in the knowledge representation language.

A third factor in deciding on an intermediate representation is the structure of the task itself and the typical way of representing this structure. If the expert has used a particular formalism whether symbolic or graphical, the knowledge engineer is advised to utilise this or an adaptation of it as an intermediate representation. A graphical or symbolic analogy is always a useful stage in any case; one which models the structure of the task and/or structure of the knowledge representation language is doubly useful. Examples of the intermediate representations as used on the ALVEY EMEX project may be found in chapter 11.

This intermediate graphical representation should be the beginning of the major analysis process. The expert task should be broken down to its basic processes. This endeavor to find the primitive operations is facilitated by listing every action, step and inference which the expert reports or the knowledge engineer infers. Document everything which may or may not be useful. It is better to include duplications, redundancy and superfluous concepts than omit important actions, faults or concepts. The knowledge engineer then discards from the analysis those actions or operations which play no part in the task currently under consideration. After this, the known parameters or conditions for each operation are documented with the relevant operations. Concepts are given 'working' (i.e. programmable) definitions. The structure of the task is represented as the linking of the major phases of the current sub-task under investigation.

The knowledge engineer is now in a position to draw up the 'rational task analysis'. This is a description of the task, without problems or errors and in the simplest form, represented as an ordered script. Each element in the rational task analysis is investigated to discover its sub-task structure down to the primitive operations. This task breakdown is represented as an and/or tree. The specifications for the primitive operations should be represented as structured English. Structured English is English which is refined to remove all ambiguities and inaccuracies.

The rise in popularity of object-orientated or frame-based systems provides the knowledge engineer with the opportunity to represent the objects which are manipulated or modelled by the expert system in a format as close to the implementation language. Five important factors must be considered when building up the model of the system in terms of the objects which the expert has suggested populate the domain. Firstly, each object must have a name, a specific identifier by which the information that object contains is accessed or modified. If there are many basically similar objects existing simultaneously, then an unambiguous method of referring to a specific entity must be chosen, as well as methods to refer to all entities of a specific type. Secondly, objects are structures which contain information dealing with many different attributes. The name of each attribute must be decided upon and any limits, or restrictions on type or value, specified. Thirdly, objects must be organised with specific links to other objects and rules formulated which detail the conditions for building these links. Fourthly, a system of inheritance is developed with sub-objects inheriting the structure of attributes, values and links from stereotypical objects. On completion of the above stages a map of the system can be constructed to demonstrate the pathways by which information is transferred from one object to another. The fifth and last consideration in this object structure is to write the rules which make inferences so values may be assigned to the slots. These rules are either written in structured English or in the knowledge representation language. The structure of objects in the system is greatly assisted by an analysis of the category structure.

## KERAVNOU AND JOHNSON'S TECHNIQUES

An intermediate representation for the description of the objects which combines ease of use with representational power is the epistemic net recommended by Keravnou and Johnson (1986). The epistemic net is used to define a concept or classify and relate entities into some logical structure.

The principle underlying the epistemic net is of selection based upon existence of one or more prior conditions. There are four classes of selection. These are shown in Fig. 8.1.

The curled arrow in the fourth example in Fig. 8.1 denotes a repeated selection: without it 'D' would be selected once. The power of the epistemic net comes in relating the separate and distinct characteristics of an object under the same heading which is in fact the same principle as the frame. Here is an example of a chess piece as represented by an epistemic net.

If control in the expert system is sensitive to changes in the status of different objects then another one of Keravnou and Johnson's representations, the status transition diagram, may well be useful. The status transition diagram, represents a high level description of procedural infor-

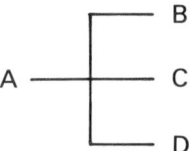

1. If A then select B or C or D

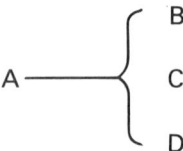

2. If A then select B and C and D

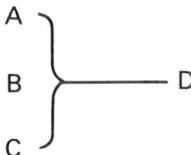

3. If A and B and C then D

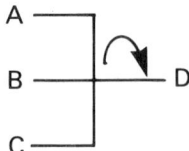

4. If A or B or C then D

Fig. 8.1 — Epistemic net.

mation. To draw a status transition diagram, firstly, identify the entities to be manipulated from the document set then list the status which the entities can take. Secondly, list the permitted transition paths, that is, for each entity which status legally or logically follows from the last. If there are many status transition paths look for an underlying principle in order to identify the status transition paths between different categories of entities. Otherwise look at the most typical or simple transitions. Lastly determine the conditions that enable the changes from one status to the next. This may be represented as a network of object/status nodes, with permissible conditions attached to the arcs.

Two other intermediate representations recommended by Keravnou and Johnson are worth mentioning. The first, relational networks, depict the mappings between factual entities. Relational networks build up a description of how objects relate to each other. Keravnou and Johnson do not give an adequate description of how to build up the relational network; however,

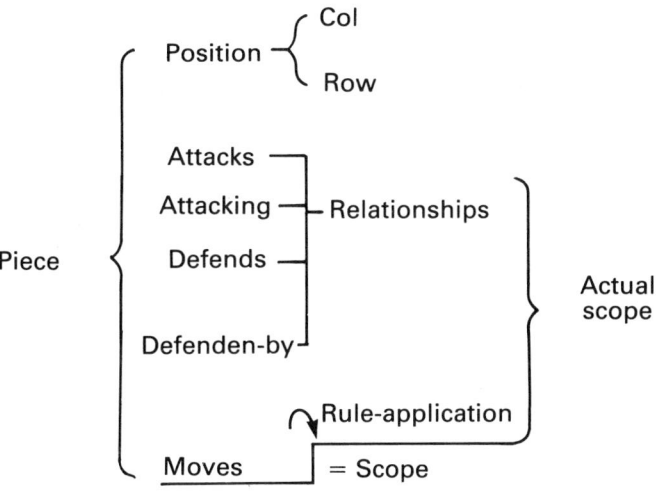

Fig. 8.2 — Epistemic net for a chess piece.

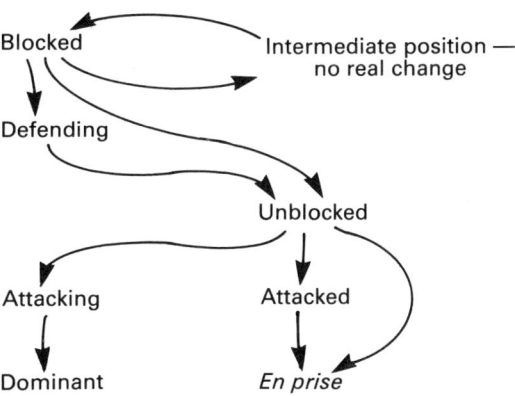

Fig. 8.3 — Status transition diagram for a chess piece which is blocked in by an opposing piece.

the author has found the following technique to work in the domains he has studied. First of all, identify the overall relationship which the network is to define. Then take the minimum number of entities, hopefully two, which are involved directly in this relationship. Associate these entities with one another and detail the connections. Relevant entities are added to the network if their relationship extends the description. The completed network should fully describe a concept in terms of the relationships between relevant entities.

Lastly, the task analysis tree which was referred to above as an and/or tree. Keravnou and Johnson detail an addition to this representation in the form of enabling or disabling conditions for the selection of tasks. Three types of condition exist: the enabling condition, the disabling condition and the relaxation condition. The presence of the enabling condition in the absence of a disabling condition will mean the task or operation is performed. A task or operation is suppressed in the presence of a disabling condition and in the absence of a relaxation condition. The presence of a relaxation condition overrides the disabling condition but is not enough in itself to cause the task or operation to be executed.

Relaxation conditions may be seen as violations of the standard requirements for applying strategies. These intermediate representations should be adequate to describe a task so specifications of the knowledge-base either can be written or can be translated directly into the knowledge representation language.

The production rule is a common type of knowledge representation. Its use in knowledge engineering has been widespread, but the power of such a representation is limited. Nevertheless, the production rule can be a useful form of intermediate representation providing the domain does not contain too many complex objects. Quite simply, a production rule is an if–then construct and reflects the most obvious manifestations of expertise — an overt decision. An example of a production rule might be: **if the temperature is over 50 and the pressure is high then open valve number 6 and reduce the power input by 10%.** In any domain there must be many of these rules and most of them are quite easy to derive from interview transcripts or think-aloud protocols. Frame- or object-orientated systems use production rules too, so a document relating all the possible production rules is an important aid to implementation.

Traditional methods of representing ideas before coding, such as flow charts, have a limited use in knowledge engineering. However, there are applications where these intermediate representations are better than most if only because they are familiar and adequate. The same is true of the data-flow diagrams and other techniques of structured systems analysis. An additional problem with using these forms of representation is reconciling a representation which models a system in terms of the flow of data through the system and a system consisting of a flow of knowledge which somehow simulates expert procedures.

## BROUWER-JANSE AND PITT'S TECHNIQUE

Brouwer-Janse and Pitt's (1986) method of analysis structures domain knowledge by extracting the problem solving behaviours of experts directly from transcripts. The technique is specifically for the analysis of think aloud protocols or other types of detailed task report. The analysis should reveal the strategic and heuristic processes which underpin the task performance.

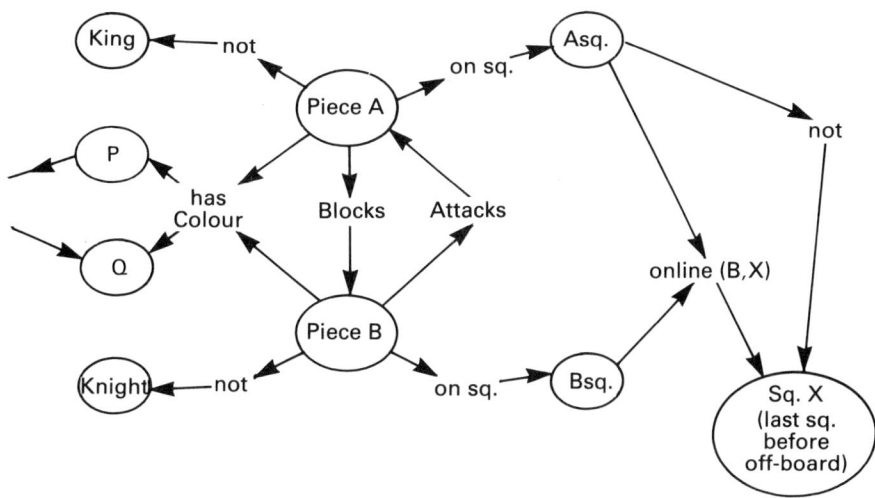

Fig. 8.4 — Relational network.

The technique analyses data at three levels. The first level deals with the identification of the elementary component processes. This requires the knowledge engineer to identify which of the 24 primitive operations are being used by the expert and in what order. The transcript is analysed into a list of processes. The 24 primitive problem solving operations as identified by Brouwer-Janse and Pitt are listed in Fig. 8.5.

The second stage in the analysis technique is to identify the heuristic sub-processes which separate the problem into three phases. The first heuristic sub-process is the act of defining the problem. The primitive operations which correspond to this phase are from 1 to 9 inclusive from Fig. 8.5. The second phase is that of data acquisition (primitive operations 10 to 18 inclusive). The final phase is of interpretation and this subsumes primitive operations 19 to 24 inclusive.

The final stage of the analysis deals with the strategic processes, of which eight were identified by these authors. These information processing functions are grouped into eight strategies shown in Fig. 8.6.

The strategies consist of a collection of primitive operations. The relationship between the primitive operations and the eight strategies is detailed in Fig. 8.7.

There are some reservations concerning Brouwer-Janse and Pitt's analysis technique. It is not certain if this technique has been used to structure a realistic domain. They admit to using the technique in the well-worn and dubious comparison between experts and novices. The results of that study have little impact upon expert systems methodology and do not serve as a suitable test of the technique. Secondly, and although they appear to argue the opposite, the typology of primitives seems incomplete and also specific to a particular mode of expertise such as fault finding or diagnosis. This is a

1. List given information
2. List assumptions
3. List possible questions
4. Select evaluative criteria
5. Assign priorities
6. List or delete relevant information
7. Formulate hypotheses
8. Define predictions
9. Select relevant question(s)

10. Define initial state
11. Define goal state
12. Identify data needed
13. Identify set of available algorithms
14. Select rule/method/procedure/algorithm
15. Edit algorithm
16. Execute program
17. Identify feedback
18. Tag new information

19. Organise and compile data
20. Match data to predictions
21. Determine truth values of predictions
22. Extract patterns from data
23. Summarise relevant patterns
24. Output conclusions

Fig. 8.5 — Primitive problem solving operations.

Describing the selection of appropriate information
Evaluation, monitoring and appraisal of the reasoning processes
Creation and development of hypotheses
General problem solving
Recognising patterns in the data
Defining conditions for executing processes
Executing processes
Concluding processes

Fig. 8.6 — Eight information processing strategies.

possible strength, as their approach of identifying primitive operations and higher reasoning constructs as amalgams of these operations is commendable. Following this approach has many virtues, of which a detailed and concise discovery of basic procedures is one. The moral, in analysing the task structure, is look, list and synthesise — the typology is left to the individual. Look back at their typology and apply the same sort of rationale to a domain near you.

| | |
|---|---|
| Selection | 6. List/delete information |
| | 13. Identify algorithms |
| | 19. Organise data |
| Evaluation | 2. List assumptions |
| | 4. Select criteria |
| | 5. Assign priorities |
| | 15. Edit algorithms |
| Hypothesizing | 7. Formulate hypotheses |
| | 8. Define predictions |
| | 20. Match data to predictions |
| | 21. Determine truth value of predictions |
| GPS | 10. Define initial state |
| | 11. Define goal state |
| | 12. Identify data needed |
| Pattern extraction | 22. Extract patterns from data |
| | 23. Summarise relevant patterns |
| Condition | 1. List given information |
| | 3. List possible question(s) |
| | 14. Select procedure |
| Act | 16. Execute program |
| | 17. Identify feedback |
| | 18. Tag new information |
| Conclusion | 24. Output conclusions |

Fig. 8.7 — Information processing strategies with relevant primitive operations.

## THE INTERPRETATION MODEL TECHNIQUE

Breuker and Wielinga (1984a) put forward the interpretation model technique of analysis as an integral part of the knowledge analysis methodology. Knowledge analysis is directly opposed to rapid prototyping. They claim their approach produces less brittle knowledge-bases owing to the greater analysis of the function of the system prior to implementation, which, they say, allows for subtle and creative solutions. A managerial benefit is the construction of a document which describes the task domain in a format which is readily excessible to others thus allowing a greater flexibility with personnel.

Their methodology consists of three components. The first component is a number of knowledge elicitation methods. This book is a refinement and extension of their general approach. The second component is the identification of domain entities, which broadly falls into the category of orientation and feasibility as presented most fully in chapter 9. The final component is the interpretation of data, which follows the selection of the intended role of the system.

Once the role of the system has been defined and accepted the knowledge engineer is able to complete a detailed specification of tasks the system has to perform. In theory it should be possible to select an interpretation model from a library of relevant models and adapt it for use in the particular application. Assuming no library of interpretation models is available, the knowledge engineer himself has to structure the transcripts into an interpretation model.

An interpretation model consists of a typology of basic elements, structuring relations and a representation of the inference structure used by the expert in the performance of the task. This may be thought of as a structured glossary which captures the expert's category structure. The basic elements or top level categories are abstractions of those objects which actually exist in the domain. These top level categories take the canonical form. Thus the same object may fall into different categories depending upon the context in which it is found. A headache may be placed in the categories of symptom and by-product (of the treatment) at the same time.

After the major categories, the sub-categories or perhaps even domain objects themselves are listed. The complexity of the domain determines the number of levels which the interpretation model hierarchy will require. For example, the basic element 'symptom', depending upon the domain, may be a high body temperature or a noise from the engine. Sub-categories of symptom might be early symptoms, late symptoms, common symptoms and rare symptoms. There may be further sub-divisions of common symptoms, or that category may consist of instances of symptoms or a mixture of instances and further sub-divisions.

By a process of induction the knowledge engineer specifies the reasoning processes of the expert with reference to the basic elements in the domain. This model is tested against the actual behaviour of the expert and refined until the knowledge engineer is satisfied with the model's veracity. A later check will arise when the knowledge engineer attempts the task for himself. The first stage of model improvement is straightforward debugging — fixing the obvious errors in the model.

The next stage of refinement is termed summation, in which the interpretation model is applied to different tasks and different experts. Finally the model is specified by having details filled in.

Breuker and Wielinga provide an example taken from the domain of wine making, specifically process control with aspects of diagnostics and planning also included. From a transcript of an interview lasting three hours the domain analysis consists of the following divisions of objects, both conceptual and actual:

      physical objects
      substances
      processes
      variables
      factors
      actions

Each one of the above is broken down into further sub-divisions. Take for example 'processes', the next level of which consists of:

> fermentation
> maceration
> aroma assimilation
> oxidation
> organic transformations
> inorganic transformations

'Fermentation' is further sub-divided into 'alcoholic fermentation' and 'lactic fermentation', while 'organic transformations' consists of the sole sub-division 'infections.'

The full example taken from Breuker and Wielinga's work is included in Fig. 8.8.

Breuker and Wielinga then move from the domain categorisation to study the processes more closely using interview material and text books. For each of the processes which they identified they attempt to impose the schema shown in Fig. 8.9.

The next stage in their analysis uncovers the strategies which determine what actions are performed and the constraints upon these actions. This begins by scanning the interview material for strategic statements such as 'I want to produce a wine that keeps' or 'Better to sell early than be stuck with a wine that needs four years to rest'. Most strategic statements concern the planning process. Breuker and Wielinga describe this process as a straightforward means–ends analysis.

During the production of the wine two monitoring processes were observed. The first concerned the monitoring of the industrial processes with respect to identification or avoidance of problems, and the second related to the consistency between the planned predictions of intermediate and actual results. The monitoring process takes input evidence in the form of test results, various measurements and the status of external factors such as weather conditions. The outputs are predictions of the properties of the final products or the identification of problems.

Breuker and Wielinga are able to map out a conceptual structure which represents the planing and monitoring processes. This is shown in Fig. 8.10.

From the conceptual structure a number of knowledge sources can be identified and classified. In the areas of planning these include: production constraints, problem prevention, general heuristics and remedies.

Breuker and Wielinga conclude that their method means that a large amount of information can be gained from even a short interview. Secondly, the refinement of prototypical interpretation models using verbal data provides a structured method to construct a conceptual structure for a particular task; and lastly, the use of various categories of elements in the interpretation models structures the data and provides plans for the elicitation of data.

Objects
    physical objects
        *cuve*
        cooler
        pump
        *marc*
    substances
        grapes
        gas
            $O_2$
            $CO_2$
            $N_2$
            $SO_2$
        yeast
        must
        wine
        malic acid
        lactic acid
    processes
        fermentation
            alcoholic fermentation
            lactic fermentation
        maceration
        aroma assimilation
        oxidation
        organic transformations
            infections
        inorganic transformations
    variables
        substance variables
        sugar content
        tannine content
        aromatics
        acidity
        lactic acidity
        malic acidity
        taste variables
    process variables
        temperature
        $CO_2$ development
        heat exchange
        gravity reduction
    external variables
        external temperature
        weather season
        age of vineyard
        type of grape
    factors
        client taste
        liquidity of proprietiere
        storage capacity
        interest rate
        consumption patterns
        market
    actions
        cleaning methods
        harvesting methods
        *défoulage*
        pressing
        open/close *cuve*
        cooling methods
        *écoulage*
        $SO_2$ addition
        yeast selection
        yeast preparation
        *macérage*
        oxygen addition
        add old wine
        grape mixture
        amount of grapes/*cuve*
        stop fermentation
        perform lab tests
        add sugar (illegal)

Fig. 8.8 — The most important objects in the sub/super-class hierarchy for the domain of wine making (the expert was French).
(From Breuker and Wielinga 1984a).

Basic input substances
Product substances
Important substance variables affected
Process variables
Side effects on variables
Relationships between variables
Catalysts
Underlying chemical/physical processes
Problems

Fig. 8.9 — Schema for analysing processes.
(From Breuker and Wielinga 1984a).

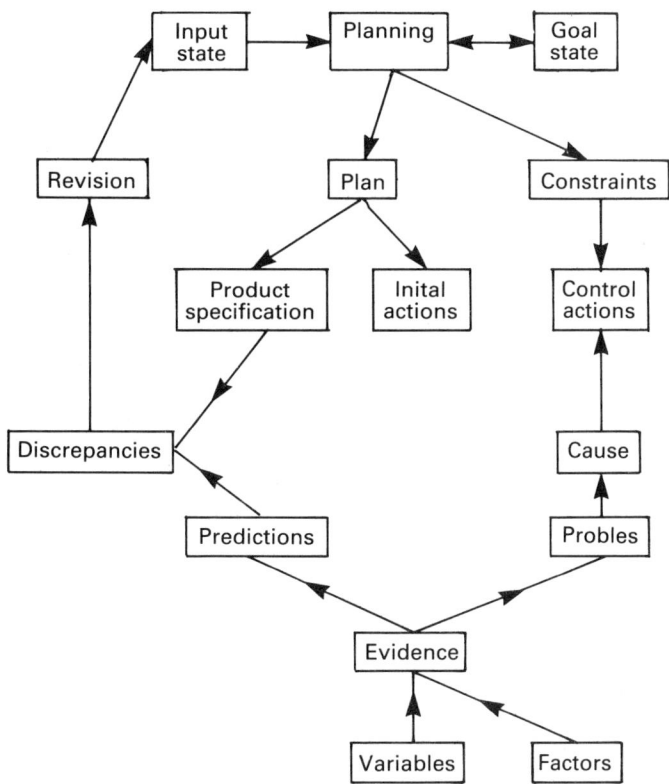

Fig. 8.10 — Conceptual structure of process control and planning in commercial wine making. (From Breuker and Wielinga 1984a).

Without investigating their transcripts it is difficult to make an objective assessment of their method. In essence it consists of two representations of the transcript data, the catalogue of domain objects and the conceptual structure of the reasoning processes. The catalogue of domain objects is a very useful document and does not require a vast amount of intellectual effort from the knowledge engineer to construct. The conceptual structure of the reasoning process is a more contentious representation and really does require the transcripts to explain how it was formulated in that particular way. We must ask the question, what is this conceptual structure and where does it come from? I have suggested previously that the expert's method must be inferred from the evidence (transcripts, think-aloud protocols, observation, etc.). That is why we have knowledge engineers and also why some people believe the knowledge acquisition process can be automated. However, it is a very creative form of inference as the inferred reasoning strategy must reside, in its dynamic form, in a representation which is very different from and much less powerful than the source representation - the expert's cognitive structures. While the need for a structured approach to knowledge acquisition and knowledge analysis is appreciated, there appears to be a problem with a structured approach to conceptualising the expert's method when some of the determinants of the conceptual model are independent of the expert (e.g. the knowledge representation, the domain, the intended complexity of the final system).

While the efficacy of the interpretation model technique may be in doubt, it does have some interesting points. The most important point seems to be the orientation towards understanding, and an understanding at a psychological level rather than an orientation towards implementation which a traditional systems analysis approach would take. Knowledge engineering must always put understanding before implementation. Secondly, the strong distinction between the domain structure, with the emphasis upon structure, and the dynamic aspects of the experts reasoning is a fundamental distinction but one which is often blurred. Thirdly, it is an attempt to unite knowledge acquisition with knowledge analysis, which is a necessary precondition for good knowledge engineering. Lastly, and some of the reservations about the technique may have to put on one side, the Knowledge Acquisition Documentation System (KADS) has emerged from the original work in interpretation models. The KADS system provides some very useful tools for knowledge analysis and represents one of the best attempts at providing software support for knowledge engineers.

## SUMMARY

- The cycle of preparation/interview/analysis is broken by a major analysis.
- An intermediate representation should adequately represent the knowledge which eases the transition to the knowledge representation language
- The more the knowledge engineer understands about the expertise the less detailed the intermediate representation need be, and vice versa
- If the implementation language has a high degree of representative power then the intermediate representation which just outlines the main ideas will probably suffice

- Frame-based or object-oriented knowledge representation languages make the representation of the domain much simpler

# 9

# Management and feasibility

**INTRODUCTION**

The project management of the elicitation phase of an expert systems project must be seen within the context of the project management of the whole project. This chapter is concerned with the management of the knowledge elicitation phases as part of the managerial techniques which were specifically designed for the construction of expert simulation systems. The scope of this chapter, and the next, is the complete project from inception through feasibility, first cut — first prototype, later cycles and finally delivery. This chapter includes an overview of the tasks which must be included within the whole project and then focuses upon the feasibility study. The tasks which must be achieved during the project are listed in Fig. 9.1.

Feasibility study
Design
Coding
Testing
Integration
Implementation
End-user training
Maintenance

Fig 9.1 — Tasks to be achieved during an expert systems project.

**SOFTWARE**

Little has been said so far on the subject of software in what is after all a software project. A knowledge engineer with responsibility for the acquisition of knowledge need not be concerned at all with coding. Alternatively, it is possible that the knowledge elicitator is also the software engineer. This chapter assumes a middle way between these two extremes — one knowledge engineer is primarily responsible for knowledge acquisition, which includes the analysis of the knowledge, and is co-responsible with others for writing the knowledge-bases. The co-responsibility also includes an input to the design of the system. The degree of involvement is determined, to a large degree, by the specific knowledge engineering environment. A greater involvement is to be expected if the project has developed a knowledge representation language specific to the domain or has a general proprietary knowledge engineering environment, that is one, designed and used solely by those who work for the organisation, or uses a commercial knowledge engineering package commonly called a shell. Unless the knowledge elicitator is very experienced in a particular computer language applicable to knowledge-based systems, the degree of involvement in coding should be low. In this situation there must be a high degree of specificity in the intermediate representation.

Three areas of software are combined in the total expert system. They are the conventional area, which largely consists of the user interface and interfaces to other software packages, typically implemented in computer languages like C or PASCAL. The second area of software is the knowledge representation language or the extensions to the knowledge engineering environment. This is usually written in a computer language such as LISP, PROLOG or POP11. And lastly, there is the coding of the knowledge itself which may use a shell or the specific knowledge representation language. It is possible for the knowledge to be directly encoded in a computer language such as LISP, PROLOG, or a more traditional DP language. There is a benefit in the speed of implementation when using a programming language for knowledge-bases. However, this benefit can be a short-term one with problems arising with the maintenance of the system. The readability of computer code does not compare well with a well designed knowledge representation language. The benefit of using hard copies of the knowledge-base as a knowledge engineering resource is inestimable. If the expert can converse about the knowledge-base it is only a matter of time and effort before she can write it. Whether or not it is preferable to have the expert writing the knowledge-base is dependent upon the particular circumstances of the project and competence of the expert as a coder.

**TASK STRUCTURE**

The principle components of the task structure are the three phases and the cycle of tasks which are performed during the main phase. The principle management resource is the documentation set, principally the statement of requirements which precedes each cycle and upon which the success of the cycle is judged. Expert systems, most certainly at the present time, are more amenable to the flexibility induced by the cyclic approach than the following of a set project plan and detailed specification. It is difficult to say if this will always be the case or whether it is a manifestation of an immature technology.

One reason for the more flexible, cyclical approach to project management is the problems inherent in knowledge acquisition. This costly process may unearth as many problems as nuggets of knowledge. Solving these problems may be the responsibility of any of the team members in any of the areas of endeavour that make up an expert systems project. Conversely, knowledge acquisition may provide opportunities which were not perceived at the outset of the project and are potentially very rewarding. The opportunities may affect the system being built, the expertise, or any of the contributing organisations. A flexible approach to the project as a whole is one which can adapt to new problems and new ideas.

The other main component of the managerial methodology, as well as a major part of the knowledge acquisition phase, is the feasibility study. This chapter concludes with an account of the feasibility study.

## THE FEASIBILITY STUDY

One of the problems with an expert systems project is the amount of optimism or pessimism which is shown by the different participants in the process. Expectations tend to change throughout the life of a project if only because all the participants tend to set their sights too high. It is the role of the feasibility study to address the issue of the expectations at the outset of the project. One function of the feasibility study is to provide the readers with information so they can reassess their initial evaluation of expert systems technology relative to their requirements. The feasibility study should demonstrate the commercial case for an expert systems approach without supporting the unrealistic expectations of the readership.

The pessimistic potential client will be a difficult person to convince. He will certainly not be convinced by unrealistic claims for the technology. It may be necessary to demonstrate the inability of conventional computer methodology to produce the desired system. Indeed if this argument cannot be made it is unlikely that an expert system solution will be acceptable under any other criteria.

The knowledge engineer should be responsible for the research for and the writing of the feasibility report. He should, if he is going to succeed as a knowledge engineer, have the necessary skills to accomplish the task. He is also in the best position to benefit from the undertaking as he establishes a working relationship with the expert as well as other significant people involved in the project, from the very beginning. The analysis of the contents of interview 1 which provides the bulk of the content of the feasibility study is the foundation of the knowledge analysis from which the bulk of the knowledge-base will arise.

If there are weaknesses in the knowledge engineer's understanding of the total software requirements for the projected system then the expertise of an experienced software professional must be called upon. Another weakness may be the knowledge engineer's appreciation of the detailed cost issues. Questions concerning money are best left to the experts in that field. However, the knowledge engineer should have a good acquaintance with the strategic issues. Strategic issues are concerned with the socio-technical effects of expert systems. These issues will become more important as more expert systems are put into commercial use. The knowledge engineer does not need to be responsible for all of the feasibility study but must take the role of coordinating various contributions to it.

This scenario may be typical of the beginning of an expert system project. An expert systems application having been identified, the knowledge engineer, after some discussion with more senior management, visits the client's company and presents interview 0, the 'this is expert systems technology' presentation. The next meeting will probably be with a contact in the client's organisation responsible for the expert system project. A sample selection of the questions which should be asked at that meeting is included at the end of this chapter. After that meeting the knowledge engineer should begin interview 1 with the expert. Lastly, when the knowledge engineer is satisfied that the potential user of the proposed system has been identified, an interview should be held with at least two prospective users. A small selection of questions which may be used at this interview are also included at the end of the chapter.

Cost is fundamental to any feasibility study, and is of equal prominence with the justification of expert systems technology as the only possible solution. Expert systems technology is expensive; however, until recently the expectation was that the same costs and times applied to expert systems technology as to more conventional information technology. Similarly, it was assumed conventional information processing technology project management techniques applied to expert systems projects too. The major reason why the cost and management assumptions are incorrect is the expense, length and complexity of the knowledge acquisition process and, in particular, knowledge elicitation. A major part of this expense is the cost of the expert which must include the opportunity cost. The opportunity cost takes into account how the expert would otherwise be employed if they were not involved in the knowledge elicitation sessions and any other duties which they might perform on behalf of the project. Although estimates of the time taken in knowledge acquisition are determined by the complexity of the domain and intended system as well as other factors it is not unusual to expect some 50–100 hours of knowledge elicitation to be required. Approximate analysis time is assessed by multiplying elicitation time by seven. Implementation and refinement will probably take twice as long as the analysis. An expert system project which takes less than a year of elapsed time is an exception.

The major difference between expert systems and conventional information processing technology is the difference between knowledge engineering and systems analysis. Whereas systems analysis is oriented to what the user wants, knowledge engineering is oriented towards the expert's method. Although systems analysts are good candidates to become knowledge engineers, knowledge engineering is not systems analysis in a different guise.

When approaching the cost issues in the feasibility report the knowledge engineer must investigate the following. Firstly, he must look for a conventional or algorithmic solution. If the complexities involved in performing the task are beyond a conventional approach then the most likely solution will be to simulate the expert's actual method. As an aside a third option is the artificial intelligence solution which is probably unwarranted with the existence of an expert. One solution which is rarely considered is to avoid a computer-based system at this time and seek an organisational solution. Assuming an expert system is seriously considered, the knowledge engineer then investigates the expert's method and decides as to its applicability with regard to acquisition and synthesis, taking into account organisational alternatives such as the employment and training of a good novice. There is a lot of guess work involved in this investigation, such as the likely running time of the system (which will probably reduce as hardware is improved) and the likely time taken by a good novice. Comparisons between efficiency and accuracy of the good novice and expert system must also be made. A factor which strongly supports the applicability of an expert systems solution is the simplicity of the expert's task in comparison to an alternative solution.

Other factors involved in calculating the total cost of an expert system must include the cost of bad advice emanating from the system or, somewhat more optimistically, the benefit of improved performance. The cost of the knowledge engineering effort must be included and this cost must be based on a realistic estimate of the time taken to complete the knowledge acquisition. Equipment costs for knowledge engineering include audio or video recording equipment suited to the task, the use of word-processing and transcribing equipment or services. The choice of knowledge engineering environment may necessitate a new and quite expensive system or adaptations made to existing equipment. The cost of specific knowledge engineering systems is easily calculated. This is a much safer route than including the development of a knowledge representation language as part of the total project. The benefit of a propriety knowledge representation language is the relevant functionality of the system in relation to the expert's task. The knowledge representation language is designed for a particular application and supports the efficient representation of the domain objects and the manipulation of those objects and probably little else besides. The knowledge representation language may need only small changes to make it applicable to other domains. Another benefit of a specific knowledge representation language is speed of execution. If a knowledge representation language developed for a particular application cannot hope to demonstrate superiority in speed of execution then there is no reason to commission the development of it. Unless, of course, a suitable knowledge engineering product cannot be found with the required functionality. In that case the contractors will have to write their own knowledge representation language and knowledge engineering environment or implement the knowledge-base in a standard computer programming language.

Who can afford to buy these hand-crafted limousines of the computer software industry? The big financial companies, oil companies, some major industrialists and the defence industry are the major league buyers. The feasibility of an expert system can not be disentangled from the recipient of the project. The company must be prepared to pay and take a gamble. This will be true for some time to come. The cost of expert systems will reduce as a consequence of better hardware, software and the consolidation of an emerging methodology. Even so, it is and will remain an expensive proposition. Remember, traditional information processing will always be cheaper if it can be demonstrated to be an adequate solution. If the task to be computerised consists of more than just fixed procedures applied to every instance then an expert system may well be required. An expert system solution may have been identified after it proved too difficult to generate a good specification for the system from an information processing perspective. In an expert systems application it is difficult to specify what the input, outputs and processes are to the expert's task because it relies on reasoning strategies, and even the expert is unaware of details. When the input→processing→output cycle is impracticable an expert systems approach is beginning to look viable.

## REASONS FOR AN EXPERT SYSTEM

Once it looks as if an expert system and only an expert system is capable of simulating the task then the subsidiary reasons for requiring an expert system should be considered. The client organisation may wish to de-skill a particular area of the expert's job. This would be the case if the expert's domain has developed so that a part of it which can only be done by the expert at the present time is restricting the expert in developing new and more profitable areas of expertise. The firm has identified this task as one which others could perform with a limited degree of expert help — and it is the role of the system to supplement this limited expertise.

An organisation may enter into expert systems as a natural development from information processing. After an area of expertise has been identified as suitable for this new technology it is added to the stock of computer-based resources. This is the Mount Everest reason for buying an expert system project — because it is there. It is also probably the worst reason for becoming involved in expert systems.

The combination of expert reasoning and computational efficiency can turn a tedious part of an expert task into a semi-automatic process improving the accuracy and speeding up the whole task. In essence any application which adds together a computer, an expert system and an expert is a strong contender for success.

Documented expertise as a management resource can be an important factor in getting the go-ahead for an expert systems project. The final system with well presented knowledge acquisition documentation is seen as vital for policy making, the consequences of which may be worth millions of pounds to the company. If this is a major concern of the clients the knowledge engineer will have to make an allowance for the extra presentational work in the knowledge engineering plan. One use of the knowledge engineering documentation set as a formalised account of the expertise is as training material within the company. Where many experts are employed by the company to perform the same sort of task, multi-expert knowledge engineering can be used to coalesce a common view from the experts. The result of this would be some standard solutions for some of the less difficult or more frequent problems.

The secondary benefits of knowledge engineering may swing the feasibility of systems with marginal benefits or those which are inherently risky enterprises. The knowledge engineering may be used as a catalyst to combine related expertise with the aim of generating new knowledge. The resulting system has been termed an expert synthesis system and the techniques for combining contributions from a number of experts is dealt with in chapter 5. A closely related alternative is to take knowledge which has certain theoretical value and use the knowledge base as a test of the consistency and validity of the knowledge where more realistic testing may be prohibitively expensive or impossible.

A factor which militates against the feasibility of an expert system is the required reliability of the system. Expert systems may give a plausible but erroneous solution in a situation where an expert would see that special factors are operating. Expert systems are unreliable because they are software projects developed by people, and people are not renowned for perfection. The imperfection of the expert's method (they get things wrong too) or the detailed description which she provides is a second reason why experts systems may exhibit unreliable behaviour. If the client company holds reliability as a major factor then it should find more experts. An expert system can achieve greater reliability than the human counterpart. This would be the case if particular tasks performed by the expert are not suitable for people, because they are repetitive or require extreme precision. The expert system will be the more reliable if the knowledge engineering can be performed, as those tasks unsuitable for people are very often the most suitable for computers.

The proof of the computerisation of the expertise is in the elicitation of the expertise. A general guide suggests that the best type of expertise for an expert systems project is one which has been refined through experience. The task for simulation should be a task which is being performed by an expert at the time the project begins. If this is not the case there may well be problems with test cases as well as expert participation and the reliance on memory. An expert systems project will require test cases — if obtaining these looks problematic then so is the feasibility of the system. If there is not a solution to the lack of realistic test cases then there should not be an expert systems project.

## WRITING THE FEASIBILITY REPORT

The feasibility study is not a value-free document. It should scream in measured tones, 'Buy this project!' If it doesn't, the project is a non-starter. The knowledge engineer is in the situation of trying to sell the idea on top of justifying its feasibility. Having identified the companies' main interests the feasibility report should be orientated towards satisfying those requirements while making a case for the other benefits of the project which may have not been realised.

The knowledge engineer at the preliminary phase presents the technology as a solution to the customer's requirements. This may necessitate a high level review of expert systems and the domain, which may be presented to the prospective clients. The knowledge engineer then performs the interviews required to write the feasibility report. Writing the report is a combination of assessing the relevant factors from a checklist of such factors and the conclusions from the knowledge elicitation.

On the acceptance of feasibility the client and the contractor must hammer out a specification of the proposed system. The major problem here is the difficulty of producing specifications of proposed expert systems. If it is easy to draw up a specification then perhaps an information processing solution would be more applicable. The specification should be very general or contain a number of options as to the range of functionality. The specification is the measure by which the project will be assessed.

The feasibility report should attempt to crystallise the reason for an expert system in one word. The most common reasons are simplicity (of the expert's method), speed (of computerisation), potential (of greater use of expert systems methodology), or archiving (of scarce skills). The chief benefits of the system should begin with a restatement of the one word justification upon which the feasibility relies. Prominence should be given to any other benefits which seem likely to follow the successful introduction of a working system.

## DESCRIPTION AND ANALYSIS OF KNOWLEDGE

Central to an expert system is the status of the knowledge. A checklist for topics concerned with this issue is included in Fig. 9.2.

The first point in the checklist is quite straightforward. On the second point, some of the reasons why someone is an expert includes their educational and training background, experience, speed and efficiency and how long they have been with the company or doing that job. Where an expert is an expert by virtue of longevity this suggests her expertise is based on status and possibly not very amenable to expert systems technology. Expertise grounded in experience in performing relevant problem solving activities is ideal for knowledge acquisition.

Point three is concerned with the expert's subjective opinion of the task. The critical question is whether the expert likes the particular task or not. If she likes it, it may be more difficult for the expert to contribute positively to losing it. The expert may hate the task but realise that this task is central to her worth to the company and without it her position in the company will be changed. The subjective relationship between the expert and the object of the knowledge engineering is a major determinant of the success of the system.

Disagreement between experts is not a disaster for the knowledge engineer. In fact it may be regarded as a possible benefit, but only if the knowledge engineer can organise procedures so that disagreements are explicitly documented. The benefit to the knowledge engineer will come in

1. What is the exact description of the task or tasks to be performed by the expert system?
2. Who is the expert, why is she an expert, what is her motivation for participating, what is her availability? What other experts have been identified?
3. What is the relationship between the expert's current duties and the task(s) to be computerised?
4. What is he likelihood of different experts agreeing on important factors in the domain? Would they be likely to agree on the solutions to the problems they are asked to solve?
5. What are the times and complexity of each phase of the major tasks the expert system is expected to perform?
6. Look at the type of expertise which is utilised by the expert. To what degree would you mark it on the following continua?

Crisp– – – – – – – – – – – – – – – – – – – – – – – – – – – – – –Fuzzy
Specialised – – – – – – – – – – – – – – – – – – – – – – – – – –General
Creative – – – – – – – – – – – – – – – – – – – – – – – – – – Procedural
Judgemental – – – – – – – – – – – – – – – – – – – – – – – –Analytical
Social – – – – – – – – – – – – – – – – – – – – – – – – Deeply-cognitive
Old– – – – – – – – – – – – – – – – – – – – – – – – – – – – – – New
Dynamic– – – – – – – – – – – – – – – – – – – – – – – – – – – Static

Fig. 9.2 — Knowledge analysis checklist for feasibility report.

implementation when he might be given some choice as to which method or combination to accept.

The timings and completion of the task may necessitate some changes to working practices. Computerisation alters the time characteristics of the tasks. Tasks which took several minutes to be performed by eye and hand may take seconds. Correspondingly, the reasoning strategies employed by the expert system may take many times longer than the expert performing the same phase. In the feasibility study the knowledge engineer will only be able to guess at such changes — but even so these estimates must be made and their consequences explored with intended users of the system. The total time the expert system takes to complete the whole job is a less significant factor. An interactive expert system which took eighty hours to reach a suitable conclusion would be a disaster if it took the expert eight hours but not if it took a team of experts six months.

More significant is the time the expert takes to complete the task allied with the degree of repetition. If the expert takes forty hours to complete the task but in that time performs only five separate sub-tasks repeated many times, then an expert system simulation should be investigated. If the expert does many different sub-tasks in forty hours then the elicitation of the whole process is likely to be a big, expensive and time consuming problem.

The descriptions of knowledge are to a degree subjective. The point of the categorisation is to gain an insight or an overview of the knowledge. Here are some pointers towards possible meanings of the terms used. The knowledge engineer must adapt these meanings to suit the domain and his own predilection.

Knowledge is defined as crisp when it is relatively easy to explain and is not confused with too many unknown outcomes or indeterminate solutions. Fuzzy knowledge is more complex with a larger number of domain specific terms. Fuzzy knowledge is replete with indeterminacy, more often than not theoretical and will be uncertain in nature with problems of verification, while the more certain, crisp knowledge is more likely to be derived from empiricism or supported by a body of empiricism.

Knowledge which is specific to a particular application is a better bet for implementation than one which is general to many different applications. Specific applications tend to be well bounded — a major benefit to knowledge acquisition and early attempts at implementation. Expertise which is spread across a number of applications offers a choice of specific application for the knowledge analysis. For example, if we are concerned with a geological risk analysis system which is meant to be very general then it is possible to choose from the exploration for oil, or gas, or gold, etc. The knowledge engineer must be convinced that this specific application is a suitable area of investigation and this choice must be made very early in the life of the project. This assumes that it is a typical application for the expert — there are test cases available in that area and the expert agrees that most of the knowledge in the wider domain is applicable to the specific application.

The next three dimensions refer to the discussion in chapter 2. Expertise based on creativity will be very difficult to elicit and implement. Procedurally orientated expertise is a safe bet in an unsure world. Judgemental expertise is within the scope of expert systems technology if the knowledge is certain rather than fuzzy. If the knowledge does tend towards fuzziness then the success of the project may be determined by the user's predilection for reliability. However, if the system has the status of a guide or ideas box rather than a hard and fast solution, the project has a chance for success.

A very social form of expertise is beyond the current capabilities of knowledge representation and manipulation. The same is not true of a deeply cognitive form of expertise. The problem here is in eliciting the knowledge. In fact a totally different strategy of using artificial intelligence solutions based on a cognitive modelling perspective is likely to be more applicable then a knowledge-based approach. Many of the task elicitation methods including think aloud protocols, can be used but the analysis and implementation differ because it is not a knowledge-base which is being constructed but a model of cognitive and symbolic reasoning processes. Cognitive models are very detailed expositions of the information processing and problem solving strategies that the modeller infers must exist in order to explain some psychological phenomenon. A typical cognitive model would be one that explained why young children make particular errors when attempting to solve simple arithmetic problems.

Old expertise is expertise which has had time to become complex, confused and segmented. New expertise is poorly documented, in a state of transition, generally untested and the subject of controversy. On balance a new form of expertise is probably slightly better for knowledge engineering as there is a sense of adventure for all participants, thus increasing the motivation of the participants and giving the knowledge engineer scope for some subtle analytical and implementational solutions. An old body of knowledge is safer but far less exciting, and possibly has some managerial problems, as vested interests have had time to solidify.

Knowledge which is constantly changing will produce problems all down the line. The greatest problems will be in the maintenance of the system. Legal systems which are at the mercy of legislatures and case law are a good example. Feasibility in respect of dynamic knowledge may rely on adapting to the changes as simply and cheaply as possible.

## TECHNICAL FEASIBILITY

Moving on from the description and the analysis of the knowledge to the technical feasibility of the system, the knowledge engineer is advised to take note of Fig. 9.3.

Details of the source of all knowledge in the system.
Synthesis of previous section on knowledge.
Implication on reasoning strategies from previous point.
What is the intended mode of the system?
What are the chief benefits of the system?
How will the system operate?
What form will the user interface take?

Fig. 9.3 — Checklist for technical feasibility.

At the feasibility stage there should be no question as to the source of all the knowledge that will be required in the system. Speculative ideas as to what methods might be used to elicit this knowledge can also be forthcoming. This follows directly from the nature of the expertise which can be presented as a synthesis of the previous section concerned with the analysis of the expertise. Most expertise will be gleaned from the experts themselves, and introductory text books and conference papers may have already been identified.

A deeper investigation of the task is required before any hard decisions can be taken on the types of reasoning strategies to be implemented. However, the knowledge engineer should have a feeling as to broad outlines of the reasoning strategies using just the data from interview 1.

The prospective mode of an expert system results from considering the analysis of expertise and the requirements of the clients and needs of the users. The descriptions of the major types of expert system modalities are presented in chapter1. The knowledge engineer should be confident of his ability to provide that modality taking other constraints into consideration. The most important constraint is the status of the expertise. There should be one major way in which the system will operate and the most likely way is interactively with the user. The user interface is determined by the programming abilities of the conventional software team, the emphases upon what is important information as suggested by the expert, the user's state of knowledge and the client's requirements. This requires a detailed analysis of the intended users from a psychological and systems point of view.

## MANAGERIAL FEASIBILITY

The managerial checklist (Fig. 9.4) is probably the most important one of all

---

Will the expert be sufficiently motivated to fully participate in the project?
Is the expert likely to be available when needed during the life of the project?
Who will be the expert for knowledge-base maintenance?
Detail real costs of the system development and future benefits.
Include opportunity cost figures for the expert as a comparison to the alternative benefits of not participating.
Include secondary benefits of the project.
Is the sub-domain for the prototype identified and, if not, will it be difficult to identify?
What implications are there on an organisational level for the introduction of the expert system?
Security issues.

Fig. 9.4 — Management checklist for feasibility report.

the feasibility report checklists. As the report is for managers, who are more likely to make the decision on managerial than on technical grounds, this section of the feasibility study must be well researched, with the relevant information correctly presented.

Most of the issues in the management checklist have been covered previously. One very important point which must be emphasised is that if you do not have an expert or will not have one tomorrow then you do not have an expert systems project. The availability of the expert to the project should be total (within some reason). Experts who are difficult to find become difficult to work with once they are found. If maintenance is an issue then the longevity of an expert is necessary. If that cannot be guaranteed then a substitute future replacement expert must be found from an early date. Lastly, security issues refer to who is allowed to change the system, and what happens to knowledge elicitation transcripts, test cases and proprietary documentation.

## THE USER

In the final checklist in Fig. 9.5 the issues concerned with the user are listed. All of these items are straightforward enough and require no further comment.

Who is the user and why is he the user?
What does the user know of the domain of expertise?
What functionality of the system will the user require?
Will the user require detailed explanation facilities?
Will the user require detailed help facilities?
Is the system intended to teach or train the user in the domain of expertise
What are the user's documentation needs?

Fig. 9.5 — Checklist on the user for feasibility report.

## QUESTIONS FOR THE CLIENT ORGANISATION'S MANAGEMENT

The questions for the client organisation and the potential user completes the suggested questions for the preliminary phase of an expert systems project. The other questions are to be found in chapter 6 where they comprise interview 1. Not all these questions will be asked. However, the knowledge engineer, when asking questions to which he believes he already knows the answer, should attempt not to lead the respondent. The knowledge engineer should be aiming to ask questions so his prior beliefs are challenged.

1. What do you envisage will be the benefits of the system? (List them in order of preference.)
2. Other than the completed system, are their any benefits of knowledge engineering which the organisation is interested in?
3. What do you see as the role of the system within your organisation?
4. What changes to the organisation are likely to follow the implementation of the expert system?
5. Who do you see as the typical user?
6. How well must the system perform its task?
7. How will the system complement the expert?
8. What working relationships will exist between client's staff and the knowledge engineer?
9. Is there an expected relationship between the knowledge engineers and your DP department?
10. What is the opinion of the DP department on this project?
11. Have you considered an information technology solution?
12. Do you accept and understand our project control procedures?
13. Have you considered the difficulties facing the project in terms of the knowledge elicitation phase?
14. What is the relationship between yourself and the expert?

15. Do see any problems concerning the availability of the expert for the knowledge elicitation sessions?
16. Do see any problems concerning the degree of participation of the expert as the project develops?
17. What is the expert's current role in the organisation?
18. What is a typical user's current role in the organisation?
19. Is it permissible for the knowledge engineer to observe actual interactions between the experts and their clients or study and discuss confidential documents with them?
20. Have you taken into account that the knowledge elicitation phase will take the expert away from her normal work for a large amount of time?
21. If we hold the interviews at the expert's place of work can it be arranged to have a setting which is as free from disturbances as possible?
22. Have you given thought to the organisational implications caused by the introduction of the proposed expert system?
23. What are the potential benefits to the expert of this project?
24. What are the potential costs to the expert of this project?
25. What are the benefits to the expert of the proposed system?
26. What are the potential costs to the expert of the proposed system?
27. What are the expected benefits of the system to the organisation?
28. What are the expected costs of the system to the organisation?
29. What are the expected benefits of the project to the organisation?
30. What are the expected costs of the project to the organisation?
31. What other solutions have you thought about as alternatives to the knowledge engineering solution?
32. What makes X an expert?
33. How reliable do you expect/want the system to be?
34. Can you give me a measure of the minimum reliability?
35. As the prospective role of the system stands, can you say if there is someone performing the role of the system at this moment in time?
36. Will there be any problem in obtaining test cases?
37. What other systems will the expert system have to interact with (hardware/software/social/organisational)?
38. Who is going to maintain the delivered system?

The first four questions are aimed at eliciting some of the wider strategic implications of the introduction of an expert system into commercial use. It would be surprising if the the clients have not thought about the implications of the specific expert system they wish to commission and expert systems technology in general. Nevertheless, the knowledge engineer can broaden this debate with his own ideas of the possible impact of the technology upon the company.

It is important to ascertain the client's concept of the potential user as well as the expert's. These should match; if they do not, some discussion will be needed.

The expectation of the system's performance is critical. Factors such as time, reliability and useability must be clearly stated. The issue of reliability must also be addressed here.

An expert system which is required to complement the expert in some way can be an outstanding success if the role of the system is precisely described. This will require a detailed analysis of the expert's expectations of the system and her interaction with it.

Question 8 is a pragmatic point. The knowledge engineer is interested in which other members of the client organisation will be working on the project. It is always possible that some computer personnel may become involved either because the system is to be interfaced to existing systems or because the company will take over maintenanceof the system at the end of the project. The ninth question is a more specific reiteration of the previous one. And irrespective of whether there will be close relationships between the knowledge engineers and the client's data-processing department the collective opinion of that department is an important factor. Data-processing departments can be concerned by what they may see as outsiders getting involved in their business.

Question 11 is important for two reasons. Firstly, if a conventional information technology solution was attempted or suggested and rejected then the way is clear for an expert systems solution. This would also suggest that the company's own computer systems people will be in favour of an expert system solution being tried. Secondly, if a conventional solution has not been investigated then the feasibility study must address the suitability of that approach and hopefully reject it. Also it is interesting to find out why an expert system was the first suggestion.

Whatever the particular style of project management to be used, the client must be aware of it, particularly if it is somewhat non-standard or is likely to require a lot of patience. On the subject of patience it is better if the client company as well as the expert are aware of the difficulties in knowledge acquisition.

Question 14 is important as it provides information on the social organisational structure within the company. A manager who had fairly tenuous relationships with the expert would not be expected to appreciate those problems which arise because of the expert's personality or her style of working. Similarly, the manager is less likely to fit in the role of confidant or ally of the expert and knowledge engineer if the need arises.

Questions 15, 16 and 17 are concerned with the availability of the expert, while question 18 attempts to define the user. If the answer to question 19 is 'yes' then this simplifies the middle stages of knowledge acquisition. Otherwise a compromise such as a role playing exercise might be suggested.

Question 20 is a reminder that some of the expert's revenue earning capacity will be lost during the project if the project is given precedence over those revenue earning tasks. The criticalness of the expert's tasks should be addressed here. It may not be possible for the expert to be available under certain circumstances.

With question 21 it should also be ascertained if the expert is available to visit the knowledge engineer.This will be more important when new versions of the system need expert criticism. Question 22 is a reiteration of the topics which may have been addressed by the first three questions. There may be a more considered reply after the intervening questions. There must be organisational changes after the introduction of an expert system and they should have been well thought out beforehand. The feasibility study must address these issues. There is no benefit in imposing an unwanted or unusable expert system.

Questions 23 to 30 are straightforward enough and should provide the majority of the cost and benefits section. Question 31 is looking for the 'good novice' alternative, that is, some other way to spend the money. Question 32 is straightforward and the answer should be 'a life time of experience'. With questions 33 and 34 the evaluation and assessment of the system is being considered. It is very unlikely that something approaching perfection will be achieved. If that is what is wanted then the system will be a disappointment.

The answer to question 35 must be 'yes', otherwise there are likely to be problems with test cases and knowledge acquisition. On the subject of test cases it is important to verify that they are available at the very beginning. Question 37 is there just to make sure that the environmental constraints are clear, and question 38 identifies the early feeling about maintenance of the system. This opinion may change as the full extent of the maintenance task becomes known.

## QUESTIONS FOR PROSPECTIVE USERS OF THE SYSTEM

1. How much do you use a computer in your work at the moment?
2. What do you know of expert systems?
3. Do you think you will be able to contribute to the way the system interacts with you?
4. If the expert system made mistakes what would that mean to you?
5. Do you want an expert system?
6. What do you know of the domain of expertise?
7. What do [terms taken from the domain] mean to you?

The work the knowledge engineer performs with the user continues throughout the project. The seven questions above provide a foundation for that work as well as providing the required information for the feasibility study. An ideal user would be one that used computers regularly and had no strong feeling about expert systems (those expectations again). It is preferable that the user should have some knowledge of the domain of expertise and be willing to learn more and adapt to this increased level of expertise.

## SUMMARY

- The feasibility study should demonstrate the commercial case for an expert system without supporting unrealistic expectations
- The feasibility of an expert systems approach should include the inability of a conventional computing solution
- The knowledge engineer does not need to be responsible for all the

contributions to the feasibility study but must coordinate the inclusion of the various pieces
- The feasibility study should include a comparison between the proposed system and a good novice or trainee expert
- The feasibility study must take account of the cost of bad advice
- If reliability is essential then an expert system may not be the answer
- The feasibility study has to be placed in the context of the commissioning organisation
- When the input→processing→output cycle is difficult to specify an expert system might be the solution
- No test cases, no expert systems project
- The feasibility study should attempt to condense the reason for an expert system into one word; simplicity, speed, potential, etc.
- The expert's subjective opinion of the task is an important determinant of her degree of participation in the project

# 10

# The management methodology

**INTRODUCTION**

An expert systems project consists of three phases. The preliminary phase deals with the feasibility of the project and is the subject of the previous chapter. The first cut phase which follows the preliminary phase begins with the acceptance of the feasibility report, comprises the most detailed project planning and results in a suitable practical demonstration of the knowledge engineering principles. This will preferably be a prototype of a significant portion of the expertise with an example of what the final system will look like. The main phase consists of a number of cycles which extend the functionality and intelligence of the early system. The main phase may begin a redesign of the prototype. The prototype will have served a useful intellectual function but should not be developed any further. Perhaps a shell was used for early prototyping that cannot be considered for more complex knowledge engineering. The progress of the project is assessed on the basis of the modifications and developments which have taken place in the previous cycle.

There are many possible project and management configurations. Here are some examples. The knowledge engineer may be employed by a software consultancy to build a system for a client organisation. The knowledge engineer may work for a large organisation which is building an expert system using expertise found within the organisation. The knowledge engineer may have an important managerial role within the data processing department or solely on the project itself. There may be a large team which could consist of members from more than one company. Alternatively, the team may be very small — one person who is responsible for developing the company's expert system strategy and may call upon the part time assistance of the data processing department.

The management of the expert systems projects may differ from the management of other projects owing to the involvement of more senior management figures. One reason for this is the large expense of the project and the general aura of excitement and interest which surrounds expert systems. In this chapter I have assumed that the knowledge engineer is not the project manager, but is responsible for the knowledge elicitation, knowledge analysis and implementation of the knowledge-base. There is also a bias towards the knowledge engineer as consultant. This is a minor point as the relationship between two organisations is not so very different from the relationship between two departments of the same company.

## WHY A CYCLIC APPROACH?

An alternative to a cyclic approach lies in the utilisation of the feasibility study as a launch pad for a single phase based on a detailed specification of the intended system. The major problem with this approach is that an expert system project entails too many unknowns at the outset. There are too many problems which can arise and which have dramatic implications. The most traumatic would be losing the expert before the knowledge acquisition was completed. The cyclic approach means that direction can be changed and solutions sought at short notice.

Expert systems project plans must develop as they project progress. It is difficult to predict the direction a project will take at the outset, problems come from many different sources — the expert, the knowledge engineer, the knowledge, areas of software, the users or management. The best form of management control stems from continuous assessment of the status of the project. This allows serious problems to be identified before they affect the progress of the project. Continuous assessment permits a certain degree of flexibility in all project areas. This is very important in those critical tasks such as knowledge acquisition which the success of expert systems technology is dependent upon. A flexible approach to the project may mean the scope can be altered at quite short notice to avoid some serious problems or to take up an opportunity which was previously not seen or seriously considered.

Continuous assessment means progress can be observed by practical demonstrations of the system, presentation of the results of knowledge engineering and the presentation of management control documentation. As one of the major contributors in the project, the expert should be involved in the continuous assessment. The degree of direction which is attributed to the expert is dependent upon many things including the management style of the project manager. It is recommended that the expert be given a reasonable responsibility in the management of the project. However, great care should be taken here as an expert who proves inefficient at project management may object to management duties being withdrawn, thereby jeopardising the working relationship built up between herself and the knowledge engineer.

With a cyclic approach the expert is able to measure the difference between each of the end of cycle versions. This snapshot effect of the system upgrades allows the expert to put the previous cycles' work into perspective. As the knowledge engineer should be using the system as a resource to obtain more information, the expert will be familiar with the current state of the system. This may well be a very disembodied version — a system within a development environment — and this makes progress difficult to measure.

When the system is packaged for its end of cycle inspection, comparisons with previous versions can be clearly made.

The impending deadline of the end of cycle is an important incentive to achieve a particular knowledge engineering goal. This periodic concentration of effort in order to produce a presentation system provides rhythm to the project. The knowledge engineer must either justify the continuance of knowledge acquisition in a particular area of knowledge or terminate the enquiries and attempt analysis and implementation.

The end of cycle is a good time for a pause for thought. This allows new plans to be made if that is thought necessary. The various end of cycle reports on the knowledge engineering including knowledge analyses, the various software tasks, organisational changes, and user considerations, such as training and documentation, provides much useful information for the management personnel who have not been involved directly with the project.

At the end of an early cycle in the main phase or perhaps at the end of the first cut phase the shell or knowledge representation language can be assessed. This assessment of the knowledge engineering software environment is necessary even if the shell or knowledge representation language has previously been quite adequate. A new domain or different application may require a particular functionality which the current environment cannot support.

If the project team have decided to create or adapt a proprietary knowledge representation language then end of cycles provide the thinking space required to discuss the extensions which should be made to this. Not all of the software engineers' proposals will be applicable or cost effective for the work in the next cycle. It is decisions of this type that will concern the management and make them appreciate planning for a specific cycle period rather than the project as a whole.

Other changes which may be made in the following cycle include changes to the knowledge-base itself. Very often the discussion between the knowledge engineer and the expert with additional input from other software and system specialists in the presence of the project management are enough for a decision to be made. Usually these changes should be of quite small scale. However, occasionally a serious design problem in the knowledge-base is discovered and this warrants a major change in the design of the system.

## BASIC PRINCIPLES OF THE CYCLIC APPROACH

A cycle time of three months is optimum for management but probably too short for fully tested software updates and knowledge engineering. One solution is to aim for three months but allow slippage of up to one month. About one week should be allowed between cycles, for thought and planning. The amount of work completed in a cycle is dependent upon the project size, the project team employed for the cycle, the proficiency of the team and the particular stage of the project. Later stages of the projects tend to be less problematic than earlier stages as the understanding of the knowledge engineer has been built up, most of the difficult software tasks have been accomplished and are in place and being used to elicit and refine more of the knowledge, and the working relationships between management, expert and technical staff are well established.

People can be reassigned after cycles or until their effort is required in a succeeding cycle. Between cycles is a time for some experimentation and discussion as well as short holidays or visits to conferences. Fitting in cycles with major conferences does allow for a complete break. In Fig. 10.1 are a list of the tasks to be performed in each cycle or particular phases.

Feasibility study
Design
Coding
Testing
Integration
Implementation
End user training
Maintenance

Fig. 10.1 — Tasks to be achieved during the project.

Integration is an important function for the project manager. Each project is made up of a number of detached tasks, for example, the software for the infrastructure including user interface, the software for the intelligent processing including dynamic knowledge-bases. Other tasks include documentation, training, and, if the system is to be a commercial project, marketing. All these tasks and others must be meshed within the project as a whole. The project manager should check that the integration goals were achieved in the last cycle and realisable goals are set for the next cycle.

The planning of the next cycle begins with the assessment of the last phase. The end of cycle report must identify what has been achieved and, more importantly, what has not been achieved and why. Problems must be identified as soon as possible and the effect on the project as a whole determined. One major task for the next cycle may be to find a solution to the problem, even if that means that the problem will not be solved during that cycle but various alternative solutions will be presented at the next cycle end for evaluation and implementation during the next cycle. This may mean that certain tasks are delayed by six months or even more. The cyclic approach is not a methodology to avoid difficult tasks; it is a methodology to identify problems, solutions and cost effective implementations in a way which ensures that the most serious of the problems are dealt with before the progress of the project is put in jeopardy. The same is true of the knowledge engineering; it is an error to attempt an implementation of derived knowledge which is unsatisfactory, for whatever reason. Knowledge elicitation approaches and the products thereof are important subjects for review at the end of early cycles.

The detailed planning of the succeeding phase begins with the decision as to what improvements can be made to particular software areas including the additional software features. These improvements may assist the project, improve system performance or user interface, or extend the scope of the knowledge-base. Management must decide what refinements and improvements are needed to the knowledge-base, what tasks have been put off and must be completed before the end of the project.

## MAJOR STAGES WITHIN THE CYCLE

Each cycle begins with the end of the previous cycle. The overlap consists of the demonstration of the work achieved in the previous cycle. Obviously, a new system is pivotal in this respect but other areas should demonstrate progress too. Draft copies of documentation, training schedules and report backs from user groups should be presented, as well as any increased functionality with respect to performance on the test cases being demonstrated.

The management and technical staff should have in their possession the reports which detail what progress has been made in the previous cycle and what work is planned or options available for the next cycle. The appreciation of the current status of the project can be enhanced by an open discussion of the end of cycle reports and the general direction of the project. This should be followed by a period of reflection in which plans and decisions are made as to the actual nature of the work to be carried out in the next cycle. The tangible result of this contemplation is the statement of requirements for the next phase. This document should of course be adapted from previous cycles. Also a project plan for the phase is drawn up to achieve the goals set down in the statement of requirements.

The first task for the technical staff is to enact any trivial changes to the last cycle system which are requested by the current statement of requirements. This may include changes to the wording of questions, or refinements to the rules in the knowledge-base. The next task for the technical staff is to make the alterations to the design which are called for to accommodate the changes suggested by the statement of requirements. As the system develops there should be fewer major changes to the basic infrastructure software and more changes to the knowledge-base as the system is now more able to demonstrate its functionality and intelligence. Anything more than trivial changes should be approached with care. The complexity of these systems mean a change to one area has unpredictable effects which ripple through the system and are often the cause of unprecedented havoc as the system fails where it was once sound or starts showing eccentric behaviour.

The task of extending and refining the knowledge-base is a major part of the cycle. Its first stage is the elicitation and analysis of any new objects, rules and procedures. This is followed by the implementation of the knowledge analysis. As previous chapters have stressed, elicitation, analysis and implementation are not independent. No more need be said on this subject as most of this book has been devoted to knowledge acquisition. As the end of the cycle becomes imminent those items included in the statements of requirements which have not been implemented or have been awaiting the completion of an earlier task become priorities. This may be in any area of the project, software or support.

The knowledge engineering progress must be checked against test case performance. Test cases have two roles in the expert system project. In their technical role they are used to check the changes to the knowledge-base at all stages. In their managerial role they provide explicit continuity from one cycle to the next. This does not mean that test cases must always show an improved performance but hopefully, never a degradation of performance. Test cases, as a knowledge engineering resource, demonstrate the reasoning processes used by the system. The reasoning trace may only be obtainable and understandable to the knowledge engineer, and may show errors that would go unnoticed by observing the test case results only. The test cases or the analysis of the reasoning strategies may demonstrate a mis-specified knowledge-base. It is very unlikely that the knowledge-base does not include some bugs. Debugging the knowledge-base is one of the final tasks in the cycle.

Finally, preparations must be made for the end of cycle demonstration and the end of cycle reports to be written. The final task in the cycle and the first in the new cycle is the demonstration itself.

The major stages are summarised in Fig. 10.2.

1. Demonstration at end of last cycle
2. Project planning and writing of statement of requirements
3. Trivial changes and bug-fixing in last demonstration system
4. Design alterations and changes to the infrastructure
5. Elicitation and analysis of knowledge
6. Implementation of knowledge analysis
7. Tasks awaiting infrastructure or knowledge base changes
8. Test case analysis
9. Knowledge-base debugging
10. Preparation for end of cycle
11. End of cycle demonstration

Fig. 10.2 — The Cycle Breakdown of tasks.

## THE PRELIMINARY PHASE

The work required for the completion of the feasibility study, the bulk of which is done in the preliminary or orientation phase, is presented in chapter

9. The preliminary phase is important for the management of the project as well as crucial to the knowledge engineering. If the roles are not combined in the same person, the work in this area should be shared between the knowledge engineer and the project manager.

There are five main objectives in the preliminary phase: to identify the users and their requirements as opposed to the supposed user requirements, to identify the function and mode of the system most suited to the environment and user, to ascertain how the project can be accomplished, to identify evaluation criteria and finally to sell the idea to the client or one's own organisation. The information required for completion of these objectives is obtained by performing a series of interviews, examples of which are presented in chapter 7 and chapter 9.

The work at the preliminary phase can be sub-divided into three headings. The first heading is requirements. The first division consists of a high-level review of the domain and the strategical effects of different proposed systems. This should be presented as a written report and if possible a stand-up presentation with coloured slides and 'bubble diagrams'. The report should summarise the detailed interview material and also include a more detailed analysis which approaches knowledge engineering documentation. The second heading is feasibility. This is the result of applying the information presented under the last heading to analysis by use of a number of checklists and has already been covered. The third heading is the knowledge engineering. This is the more detailed analysis of the work which was included under the requirements section and from which some of the requirements section will have been derived. This work forms the basis of the knowledge engineering in the first cut and main phase. Thus the work in the preliminary phase consists of making contacts, setting up interviews, analysing the outcomes and writing the reports.

There are four documents associated with the preliminary stage. The first is the initial findings, Produced after first meetings with the initiators of the system and the expert, this document expresses the project benefits and the terms of reference for the detailed studies.

The second document, the detailed report on the knowledge engineering, is written after the final meeting with the expert in the preliminary stage and after the meeting with the prospective user. This document categorises and describes the suite of test cases, which experts have been identified and their roles in respect to the knowledge engineering and project, and the technical characteristics of the expertise. This final category is best presented as a mixture of a knowledge analysis formalism, such as an interpretation model (see chapter 7), and prose.

The third document emanating from the preliminary stage is the feasibility study. This is dealt with in chapter 9.

An additional document is the end of cycle report for the preliminary phase. This phase takes about six weeks to two months and is a short cycle but a cycle nevertheless. The end of cycle report coupled with the presentation gives everyone a chance to appreciate the way the project is to be run. The end of cycle report on the preliminary stage should include a statement of the project objectives, a statement of requirements, the specification of assessment criteria, the specification of required conventional software and the workplan for the first cut phase.

## THE STATEMENT OF REQUIREMENTS

The statement of requirements sustains the direction of the project. From its initial formulation in the preliminary phase it is constantly modified to adapt to difficult problems and emerging opportunities. It describes in detail the desired functionality of the system and the scope of the expertise with which the system is endowed. The latter requirement cannot be adequately stated without reference to expected levels of competence in particular areas. This is usually done by referencing the suite of test cases as suitable trials of the systems intellectual power. Decisions regarding the functionality of the system must bear in mind the prospective and identified user and the installation environment including other systems to be interfaced to the expert system. Particular attention must by paid to help and explanation facilities. Help facilities can exist at different levels: a general tutorial in the domain of expertise, a tutorial on operating the system to help on each question and each solution or sub-solution. Explanation facilities, while part of the mythology of expert systems, are very difficult to implement so they provide meaningful and useful information to the naive user.

Requirements such as training, documentation and technological awareness must also be included in the statement of requirements. Training in the use of the system could be a task to be shared by the expert and the knowledge engineers. This will depend upon the intended user's knowledge of the expertise. Documentation will probably be the sole responsibility of the knowledge engineer or preferably a technical author. Clients should specify exactly what they want in the way of documentation as this is historically an area of great disappointment in the computer world. Any strategical or marketing issues which will arise during the project should also be stated, especially so, if they involve the knowledge engineer.

## THE FIRST CUT PHASE

The first cut phase, as the second phase in the expert systems project, consists of one cycle. It begins after the acceptance of the feasibility report and statement of requirements. The first task in this phase for the knowledge engineer is to review the project documentation and source materials. The knowledge elicitation plan is drawn up and this contributes to the project plan. The software involvement in the first cut phase is quite low. A limited knowledge engineering software system is required for the first prototype. One alternative which may be considered here is the use of a shell for the first prototype. In the final system a specific knowledge representation language tailored to the structure of the domain objects and reasoning patterns is preferable. However, the expense of developing and maintaining bespoke systems is a disincentive against following this path.

The time taken to complete this phase will probably be about 6–8 weeks. It may take a little longer if a basic knowledge representation language has to be designed and developed. One of the purposes of the first cut cycle is that it gives the participants a chance to change their minds before they are too involved, even to the point of pulling out of the project. The first cut phase acts as a check on the unfounded expectations of all the participants to the project.

Review preliminary phase work
Draft knowledge acquisition plan
Draft project plan
Choose knowledge engineering environment
    or write basic knowledge representation language system
Knowledge acquisition/analysis
    (including prototype test case elicitation)
Design possible user interfaces
Prototype implementation
Write end of cycle reports
Demonstration of system and possible user interfaces

Fig. 10.3 — Tasks to be carried out in the first cut.

## TWO WAY DESIGN PRESSURES

There are two competing strategies to create computational solutions: the conventional or algorithmic and the knowledge-based. The algorithmic solution is well-bounded and predicable; the knowledge-based solution is poorly defined and less predicable. The major difference between the two is the difference between systems analysis and knowledge acquisition.

Generally the algorithmic should be used as the first attempt to understand a particular problem. If this attempt fails or is unsatisfactory then a knowledge-based solution should be tried. It has been stated in a previous chapter that the conventional solution will always win out over the knowledge-based solution on cost and therefore conventional solutions should always take precedence over a knowledge-based solution. However, some problems are of a very complex nature and it is this degree of complexity which requires the knowledge-based solution; the conventional solution will not solve the problem. This is expressed in Fig. 10.4.

In the diagram, project cost is on the x-axis and overall problem complexity is on the y-axis. With less complex problems the conventional solution is always the most cost effective. This is true until the project reaches the complexity limit — at this point the conventional solution will not provide a system of the required functionality. The only possibility is to use the more expensive knowledge-based approach.

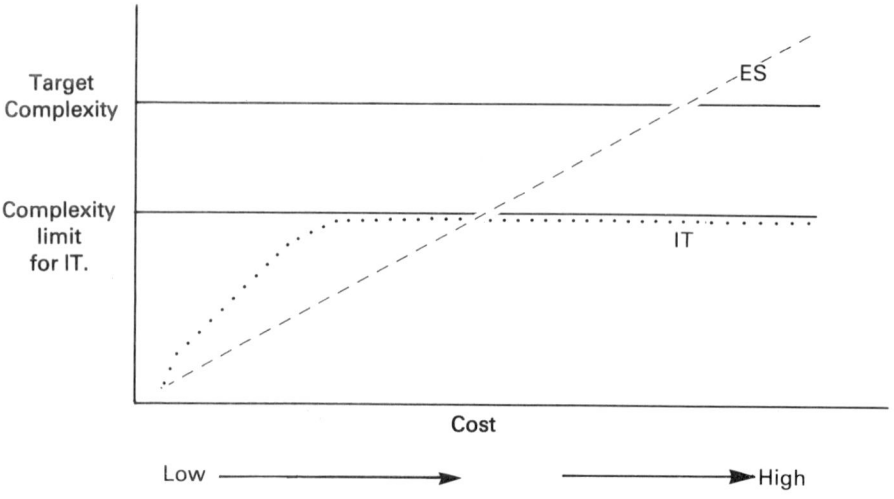

Fig. 10.4 — Expert systems can handle more complex tasks but at a greater cost.

An expert system does not always have to consist of expert method and nothing but the expert's method. There is likely to be a mixture of the algorithmic, that is, a computer science solution, and some sort of cognitive modelling solution. During a project there is always a strong cost pressure to move from a knowledge-based solution to an algorithmic solution. This is a pressure which the knowledge engineer should resist. The project management should resist this pressure too although for commercial reasons they must be more flexible.

The pressure away from knowledge-based solutions reflects the lack of familiarity of knowledge engineering. The costs, time scales and limitations of conventional software technology are well known. There is a reliance upon the knowledge engineers which makes other members of the project team uneasy. The knowledge engineer can often produce a powerful ally in any project discussion meetings — the expert, if the expert has come to accept the benefits of knowledge engineering. They will argue that the only way the method of the expert and the software media can be reconciled is through knowledge engineering. Other members of the team understand the software but only the expert and the knowledge engineer understand the method of the expert.

Those factors which push the project towards the adoption of algorithmic methods are the cost of non-algorithmic solutions, the unpredictability of knowledge-based solutions in cost and time, the familiarity of algorithmic methods, the confidence put into algorithmic solutions, the requirement for a greater common understanding of direction and ease of communication among the non-knowledge engineers on the team and the reduction of the design effort. A movement away from the knowledge-based solution is a move away from the benefits of knowledge engineering. Only where these benefits can be identified can the opportunity cost of an algorithmic solution be demonstrated. This is the only disincentive to an algorithmic approach. If an algorithmic approach is applicable then it will be cheaper.

## THREE AREAS OF SOFTWARE

In any expert system there are three areas of software which must be integrated. They include the conventional programming, which represents the user interface and any support package such as an independent module which supports complex statistical functions, the knowledge representation language, which is itself a computer program of moderate to great complexity, and the knowledge base.

Any conventional software which needs to be written or code which represents an interface to an already pre-existing package should provide few problems. The specifications for this software are unlikely to change throughout the length of the project. The first cut may see the design and most of the coding of the conventional software, with the debugging and integration being completed in the first cycle of the main phase. An alternative is to have a small conventional software team which designs, codes and integrates various peripheral packages as the project develops. However, there is unlikely to be such a high demand for conventional software, to warrant this. Conventional software would probably be written in a language such as C, PASCAL or FORTRAN. The programmers required to code up in these languages tend not to be the same people as those who build the knowledge engineering support environment and the knowledge-base. Depending upon individual company policy it is more likely that contractors would be hired to write the more conventional code or programmers from another department brought in for the duration of the work.

The knowledge representation language and knowledge engineering environment represent a major software effort. The programmers tend to be fairly rare and quite expensive to hire. The object language is LISP, PROLOG, POP11, one of the LISP object-orientated languages such as OPS5, or LOOPS. Occasionally, a more conventional language may be used such as PASCAL or C. The knowledge engineering environment tends to settle down during the early cycles of the main phase. However, a complete re-write between first cut and main phase is not unusual. The designers and implementers of this software should always be on hand throughout the project as fine tuning may be required to accommodate changes in the knowledge-base.

The writing of the knowledge-base is a less technical but a more esoteric process and is best performed by the knowledge engineer who elicited the knowledge. This is a strange mixture of concepts from programing, such as iteration and datatypes, with terms and concepts from the domain of expertise and psychology as a model of the reasoning processes are built. This software development represents the major software task and is one that runs throughout the whole of the project. It should be remembered that a propriety knowledge representation language requires a period of learning by those not involved with the development of it. It may take up to a month before the knowledge engineer is proficient in the formalism. It must be noted that this is just as true for a complex shell or commercial knowledge engineering tool.

One of the most problematic of all knowledge engineering tasks in the attempt to write a knowledge-base in a knowledge representation language which is itself still in a period of development. A functioning knowledge-base is the only definitive test of the knowledge representation language. Allowances must be made for curing some of the bugs in the knowledge representation language which are shown up by the knowledge-base. Changes to the knowledge representation language may well force changes to the knowledge-base which will lose some of the previous work.

Many project managers prefer to avoid committing resources to producing a knowledge representation specific to the domain and opt for a shell. That decision must be made on the basis of the complexity of the domain, the development and target hardware systems and the knowledge engineering packages which are available for that particular hardware. In recent years development and delivery on personal computers has been shown to be feasible and consequently a number of software packages have been available for these machines. Expert systems are no longer the sole possession of main-frame, supermini or single-user workstation owners.

The reasons to chose a shell are as follows. Firstly, it exists from day one as a functioning and supported software package, thus eliminating any delay while software engineers grapple with the inevitable and almost obligatory problems in writing their own knowledge engineering environment. The immediate availability of the system reduces the time it takes to get the first prototype running. The design of a proprietary knowledge engineering environment can await the preliminary and first cut stage knowledge analysis. In essence, using a shell usually means more to show in a shorter time and at less cost.

The author admits a certain amount of bias against using or relying upon shells as the main knowledge engineering environment. The reasons to be cautious are, firstly, unless the knowledge engineer is familiar with the shell or someone on the project team has experience or strong feelings about particular packages then the decision as to which one to use is not trivial, possibly demanding some research before an informed decision can be made. This decision is more critical if the shell is intended to be used throughout the project. If the package which is to be used is new to the knowledge engineer then there may be a reasonably long learning curve in coming to terms with the functionality of the knowledge representation language and the development environment with respect to the domain of expertise, a problem which is enhanced by the lack of any programming text books such as those which tutor the programmer in a computer language.

A shell may restrict the system to a particular piece of hardware. It is also possible that a shell may restrict the system in terms of the user interface which is available and possibly any ancillary packages which must be used by the expert system. The use of a shell may distort the knowledge analysis towards the restricted forms of implementation. The limitations of the shell start to dictate the direction of the knowledge analysis.

One of the benefits of a proprietary knowledge representation language is it can develop not only during the lifetime of the current project to facilitate the deeper recesses of the domain but for other projects and other domains. Such proprietary knowledge representation languages can be a great asset to the knowledge engineering department and are well worth the investment. To sum up, using a shell may mean less in total with an inbuilt resistance to change. Whether or not a shell is to be used for the final system, it can make a very useful contribution to the estimation of feasibility and may be carried on and used as the basis of the first cut system.

## ASSESSMENT AND EVALUATION

Expertise is a social construct and has a social role. This is a role that the expert system will have difficulty emulating. If only because a social role demands social knowledge of a type which is extensive and perhaps not publicly recognised or is under-specified. Whatever it is, it is not the stuff of knowledge-bases. For example, a client may visit an expert for an opinion on a particular scheme they have in mind. The expert considers the idea and replies that what they want to do is feasible and quite legal but because it does not conform to the spirit of some particular convention there will be problems. The expert confides to his client that there are unwritten methods of delaying and frustrating schemes such as the one they are proposing which the authorities may well use. This is the manifestation of pure expertise. Not only does the expert know or seem to know everything about whatever you want to know — they know a little bit more too.

Assessment then, taking the above example into account, begins by defining the limits of the systems performance from the social perspective, taking into account the role of the users. With the social role of expertise isolated, the dynamic and intelligent aspects of the system can be evaluated. The central indices are the test cases which should be chosen with respect to their typicalness and to the extent they represent an adequate test of the system's abilities. A much clearer metric is the technical criteria of successes such as, 'does it run on the right machine?' and 'is the processing time adequate?'. A system may pass all the technical examinations and still fail the most important one — is it usable? This can only be ascertained by observing interactions between the system and the end user and analysing the results. This evaluation should always originate from outside the development team, and that includes the expert. A large part of this evaluation will be concerned with the user interface, although the additional functionality such as the explanations of reasoning, instructional help text and interfaces to other commercial packages influence the user far more than the marginal status of these features suggest.

Occasionally the impact of the functioning expert system within the work place must be assessed. A very powerful and very usable system may be the square peg in the round hole from an organisational point of view. The placement of an expert system in a work place environment may cause subtle but significant changes in working relationships and disruption to finely tuned commercial, social and organisational systems. A great deal of research is needed in this area at the present time. Assuming the system is usable the final evaluation must be, 'was the project within budget?'.

The history of expert systems has not been one of unmitigated success. At the time of writing the considered opinion is that most expert systems projects have resulted in failures. The failure of these projects has been for non-technical reasons although technical problems did contribute to many of the early failures. A problem which is being overcome is the management projects that look like typical software projects but have enough differences to make conventional software management techniques invalid. The techniques of eliciting knowledge have developed to the point where if used with imagination and intelligence they should do the job. The techniques of managing knowledge engineering are still developing and this chapter represents a brief introduction to just one of the emerging perspectives. There is more to be discovered.

## SUMMARY

- There are three phases to an expert system project: the preliminary phase, the first cut phase and the main phase
- The the first cut prototype serves a useful intellectual function and should be discarded when the main phase begins
- A cyclic approach means flexibility
- The end of each cycle gives everyone a snap shot of the current status of the project
- The impending deadline of the end of cycle is a powerful incentive
- The end of the cycle is the time at which everyone can pause for thought
- The knowledge engineering programming environment should be fully evaluated at the end of an early cycle
- A cycle time of three months is optimum with one week between cycles
- The functions to be achieved during the project are: feasibility study, design, coding, testing, integration, implementation, end user training, maintenance
- Work at the preliminary phase is divided into three headings: requirements, feasibility and knowledge engineering
- There are four documents associated with the preliminary stage: initial findings, report on the knowledge engineering, feasibility study and the end of cycle report
- The statement describes in detail the desired functionality of the system
- The main goal of the first cut phase is a working prototype
- There is always a strong cost pressure to move towards an algorithmic solution
- Three areas of software are involved in an expert system project: conventional software (user interface), the knowledge representation

language which includes the inference engine and finally the knowledge-base itself
- Using a shell usually means more to show sooner with less cost but an inbuilt resistance to change
- The decision of which shell, toolkit or knowledge engineering environment is a very important decision
- A shell may restrict the system to a particular piece of hardware
- A shell may distort the knowledge analysis towards a restricted form of implementation
- A proprietary knowledge representation language can be a great asset to the knowledge engineering team if it is sufficiently general
- The best assessment of the system or status of the project comes from someone who is independent of the knowledge engineers and experts

# 11
# EMEX: a case study

## INTRODUCTION

A case study is a natural way to emphasise and reiterate some of the ideas introduced in the previous chapters. This chapter presents examples of the management and knowledge engineering from the ALVEY EMEX project. The EMEX project is an ideal case study as the result of two years development, is a usable system, and moreover the project utilised many of the techniques of management and knowledge engineering which have been presented in earlier chapters.

The function of EMEX (also the name of the expert system) is to assist a market analyst to build an econometric model of a specific product. An econometric model is an equation which equates historical data for one of the factors (e.g. sales of a product) against the historical data for other factors (e.g. the price of the product and advertising spend, etc.). The resulting equation is an attempt to specify the causal relationships between the explained factor (sales) and the explanatory factors (price and advertising, etc.). A model may describe either the volume of sales for a product or its market share. While market specialists have a great deal of knowledge about which factors effect a particular product's performance in the market, they generally do not know how to build, or interpret, econometric models. The EMEX system simulates an expert's model building behaviour and uses as data the user's expectations and knowledge of the market and, of course, historical data. The result is an equation/model and simplistic, but useful, facilities to interpret the model. EMEX interfaces with a statistics package as the expert would: writing programs in the statistics system language and then running these programmes in batch mode. The results from the statistics package are used to activate expert procedures or are presented as output.

The ALVEY club concerned with development of EMEX consisted of those organisations listed in Fig. 11.1.

## THE MANAGEMENT

A steering committee was drawn from the club members to direct the club and oversee the development of the system. To facilitate the steering committee's task monthly reports were submitted by the knowledge engi-

Asda Stores
ICI PLC
J. Walter Thompson & Company Ltd
Sperry
Jaguar Cars Ltd
Electricity Council
United Biscuits (UK) Ltd
Henley Centre for Forecasting (contractor)
Expert Systems International (contractor)
Shell International Petroleum Co. Ltd
Procter and Gamble Ltd
Allied Vinters Ltd
Leeds Permanent Building Society
Cadbury Schweppes Ltd
British Telecom
Davidson Pearce

Fig. 11.1 — The membership of the ALVEY EMEX club.

neers. Although a monthly report is a useful guide to progress it is too short a time to assess the success of the current cycle. The ALVEY club held a general meeting at the end of each cycle to assess progress. This consisted of a presentation from the contractors and reports from the steering committee as well as a demonstration and delivery of the latest version. There was no explicit end of cycle report as such. The divergence from the management methodology presented in chapter 10 is due to the ALVEY club format. This divergence is of minor significance.

The close relationship between the contractors and the other members of the steering committee reduced the formality of the statement of requirements. The knowledge engineers and experts had a clear idea of how the project was to progress and these ideas were generally accepted by the steering committee.

While it is probably dangerous to generalise from one project as to the amount of effort and likely time scales which will apply to another quite different project this sort of generalisation is preferable to pure guess-work. To minimise the amount of disparity between any project the reader may be involved with and the EMEX project the salient factors which characterise the EMEX project are presented in Fig. 11.2.

## THE PRELIMINARY PHASE AND THE FEASIBILITY REPORT

The feasibility study for the EMEX project was very positive. As this project is set to continue as a commercial enterprise some examples of the management documentation are still commercially sensitive; this includes the original feasibility study. The feasibility study was also a very 'political' document whose aim was to bring together a number of disparate or competing companies to join in a collaborative venture of a seemingly

1. The principal objective of the club was awareness.
2. No commercial software was available which could represent the complexity of the expert's task.
3. The system was targeted for the AT or the better XT personal computers.
4. The computer programing language was PROLOG2 from Expert Systems International.
5. The system would need to interface to a statistics package written in FORTRAN.
6. The entire project was constrained by a budget of approximately £250,000 and two years elapsed time.
7. A steering committee was formed from the club members and contractors to direct the medium term activities of the project.
8. The day-to-day activities and short term direction was the responsibility of the knowledge engineers and, on some tasks, the experts.

Fig. 11.2 — Characteristics of the EMEX project.

speculative nature. However, working from the original notes, I have compiled short answers to the checklists presented in chapter 9. The numbers in brackets following the headings refer to the check lists in Figures in chapter 9.

A major finding the feasibility study unearthed was that the initial conception was not the most beneficial possible application. The original idea was to build a system which could interpret econometric models such as those developed to model the UK economy by the Treasury. The knowledge engineers and the experts decided that a system could be built to perform econometrics itself with interpretation as a component of this. One reason for this change of direction was the realisation that interpretation required some knowledge which could only be gained through building the model.

**Knowledge anlaysis checklist (9.2)**
1. What is the exact description of the task or tasks to be performed by the expert system?
(a) The system should work from user expectations and historical data towards a sensible and valid econometric model and then provide some interpretations of this model.
2. Who is the expert, why is she an expert, what is her motivation for participating, what is her availability. What other experts have been identified?
(b) The experts are econometricians at HCF. They are expert by training and experience and are available. The experts are responsible for the initiation of the project and a high degree of participation is expected. No other experts have been identified.
3. What is the relationship between the expert's current duties and the task(s) to be computerised?

(c) Econometrics is an important part of their everyday duties.

4. What is the likelihood of different experts agreeing on important factors in the domain? Would they be likely to agree on the solutions to the problems they are asked to solve?

(d) Different experts are very likely to disagree on detail and emphasis. One expert has been identified as the final arbiter. There is no correct solution, just better or worse models.

5. What are the times and complexity of each phase of the major tasks the expert system is expected to perform?

(e) Econometric model building can take up to two days. The core modelling procedure takes about half of one day.

6. Look at the type of expertise which is utilised by the expert. To what degree would you mark it on the following continua?

(f)
```
Crisp        -------------------×---------- Fuzzy
Specialised  ------------------------×--- General
Creative     --------------------×-------Procedural
Judgemental  ---------×------------------ Analytical
Social       ---------×-----------------Deeply cognitive
Old          --------------------------×------ New
Dynamic      ----------------------×---------Static
```

**Technical feasibility checklist (9.3)**

Details of the source of all knowledge in the system.

(g) Reasoning strategies should be based on the procedural nature of the econometrics processing.

What is the intended mode of the system?

(h) The system should run interactively and either ask the user for information in advance of processing or request information as it is needed.

What are the chief benefits of the system?

(i) The system's chief benefits will be to perform an expert function avoiding detailed interaction with statistical software with very little knowledge of how to perform econometrics.

**Managerial feasibility checklist (9.4)**

Will the expert be sufficiently motivated to fully participate in the project?

(j) The experts are motivated, part of the management team and generally available at short notice.

Include secondary benefits of the project.

(k) As an ALVEY club, club members will experience the development of an expert systems project and gain information concerning econometrics.

Is the sub-domain for the prototype identified and, if not, will it be difficult to identify?

(l) The prototype should cover the phase of econometrics called proposing the general model.

## The user checklist (9.5)
Who is the user and why is he the user?
(m) The user is intended to be a marketing or brand manager.
What does the user know of the domain of expertise?
(n) Generally the user is aware of econometrics but has little knowledge of how to perform econometric modelling. Although some users are experienced modellers.
What functionality of the system will the user require?
(o) The users want to use models rather than build them. This may be a problem in the short term.
Will the user require detailed explanation facilities?
(p) Explanation facilities are not vitally important in this domain.
Will the user require detailed help facilities?
(q) Help facilities are very important.
Is the system intended to teach or train the user in the domain of expertise?
(r) Instruction in econometrics is a minor part of the system.
What are the user's documentation needs?
(s) Detailed documentation is very important.
(t) Users are computer literate.
(u) They know little or nothing of expert systems.

## THE FIRST CUT

The knowledge engineering on the whole project divided into two relatively distinct areas. One area dealt with the creation of a knowledge representation language and corresponding inference mechanisms. Included in this area was the infrastructure software which was the responsibility of the knowledge engineer although not always written by him. The other area included the knowledge elicitation, analysis and implementation which was my responsibility.

For the first cut phase of the project one knowledge engineer was almost totally responsible for the knowledge acquisition and the prototype implementation. However, some assistance was provided for the less complex tasks. The first prototype was written almost totally in PROLOG2. During the end of this phase the second knowledge engineer (myself) joined the team and made the following discoveries:

1. There was no knowledge engineering documentation set.

2. Other people's knowledge elicitation tape recordings do not provide a suitable medium for understanding the complexities of the domain, as expected, and certainly if the enquiries were not structured towards a general understanding.

3. Reverse engineering from the prototype knowledge-base provides little in the way of understanding the expertise (and is very boring).

4. The only way a knowledge engineer can understand the domain sufficiently and function as a useful member of the team is to perform a domain

analysis himself, taking a structured approach to this process. Discussions with a knowledge engineer who has some experience of working in the domain is still not sufficient, although it is possible that it was too early in the life of the project for a knowledge engineer to have much explanatory knowledge of the domain and that a more structured approach to the domain analysis would have increased his understanding.

5. The only saving in what was to some extent duplicating work already done by the other team member was that the feasibility study did not have to be duplicated.

6. A good domain analysis is the best foundation for successful knowledge acquisition and a successful project.

**THE MAIN PHASE**

The main phase consists of a number of similar task cycles of which Fig. 11.3 is a typical example. If the preliminary and first cut phase were successful then there should be few surprise problems in the main phase.

1. General club meeting to review progress and deliver next version
2. Review of members' comments
3. Plan next cycle
4. Make minor changes to previous version
5. Fix conceptual errors in the knowledge-base with the assistance of the expert
6. Knowledge acquisition for new section of the knowledge-base
7. Knowledge analysis
8. Review (of new knowledge-base section)
9. Integrate system (include any changes to infrastructure)
10. Test case analysis
11. Prepare for next demo/release

Fig. 11.3 — A typical cycle of tasks in the main phase.

The only major decision that had to be taken during the main phase was dropping the development of a section of the knowledge-base owing to the lack of time. This was not unforeseen as it had been predicted that too much was being expected from the knowledge engineering in too short a time.

**PROJECT COST**

The steering committee's major role was to monitor the cost of the project. This was done with exceptional success. At the end of the project it was found that there had been a 3% overspend, which for a successful software project is as close to perfection as it is possible to get. Where there were some surprises was in the large proportion which had to be allocated under the heading of knowledge engineering. As there had originally been a certain proportion allocated for system analysis, it was accepted that knowledge engineering subsumes systems analysis (whatever that term means in an expert systems project) and consequently swallowed the budget set aside for it and a little more besides.

The project expenditure is broken down in Fig. 11.4.

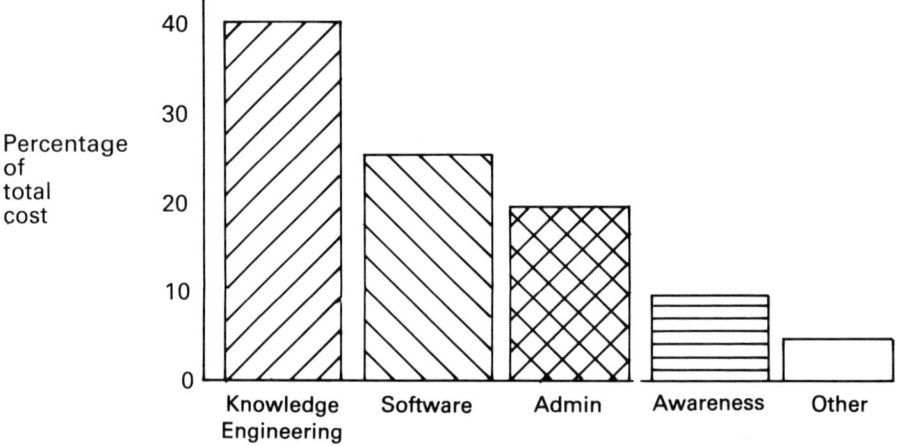

Fig. 11.4 — The EMEX Project expenditure.

## PERSONNEL

There was a very small team working on the EMEX project. Two knowledge engineers were employed full time for most of the project. Occasional PROLOG programmers were seconded for short periods during three of the four cycles in the main phase. These programmers were concerned with the help system, user interface, KRL debugging facilities and the interface with the statistics package. The knowledge engineers were to a large degree self-managing; the project manager was primarily concerned with liaison with the steering committee and other club members.

There were six experts working with the knowledge engineers. One expert had a high status in his organisation and took on the role of final arbiter with respect to any disagreements among the other experts. Each expert supplied one test case, and took part in interviews with the knowledge engineer when available. The personnel and their roles appear in Fig. 11.5.

1 knowledge engineer
    — PROLOG software
    — system design
    — knowledge-base design                               full time
    — (awareness) writing working papers
    — compiling monthly reports

1 knowledge engineer
    — knowledge elicitation
    — knowledge-base design
    — knowledge representation language programming     full time
       (from 1st cycle main phase)
    — (awareness) writing working papers

1 project manager
    — ALVEY liaison,
    — checking progress                                      10 hours/month

1 head expert
    — ALVEY liaison
    — knowledge elicitation
    — prototype/version criticism                          15 hours/month
    — (awareness) writing working papers

1 PROLOG programmer — interface stats package   2 months full time
1 PROLOG programmer — help system              1 month full time
1 PROLOG programmer — user interface            2 months full time
1 PROLOG programmer — KRL debugger            1 month full time

5 experts
    — knowledge elicitation
    — test cases
    — help text
    — prototype/version criticism
    — econometric workshops
    — some ALVEY liaison

Fig. 11.5 — Responsibilities and commitment of the personnel.

Fig 11.6 shows which knowledge acquisition techniques were used within each cycle and at each phase. The major tasks which correspond to the cycles are also included with the elapsed time and effort required to complete the

| Date, phase and major tasks | Knowledge elicitation methods |
|---|---|

Oct. 85–Jan. 86
1. Preliminary phase
feasibility study

structured interviewing
observation

This phase took 4 months' elapsed time and required 2 months' effort.

Feb. 86–Jun. 86
2. First cut
knowledge elicitation
building prototype in PROLOG
writing help text

structured interviewing
focused interviewing
think aloud protocol review

The first cut cycle took 5 months' elapsed time and required 12 months' effort.

Jul. 86–Sep. 86
3. Main phase (1st cycle)
analysis of prototype criticism
knowledge elicitation
design of knowledge representation
    language and EMEX environment

structured interviewing
focused interviewing
observation

This cycle took 3 months' elapsed time and required 8 months' effort.

Oct. 86–Dec. 87
4. Main phase (2nd cycle)
implement knowledge representation
language
detailed knowledge elicitation
writing two sections
    of the knowledge-base

focused interview
think aloud protocol
observation
teachback user analysis

This cycle took 3 months' elapsed time and required 9 months' effort.

Jan. 87–Mar. 87
5. Main phase (3rd cycle)
integrate user/stats interface
detailed knowledge elicitation
writing one section of knowledge-base
debug/extend previous sections

focused interviewing
version criticism
think aloud protocol
on test cases

This cycle took 3 months' elapsed time and required 10 months' effort.

Apr. 87–Jul. 87
6. Main phase (4th cycle)
writing two sections of the knowledge-
    base
consolidation of knowledge-base
debugging
documentation

focused interviewing

version criticism

This cycle took 4 months' elapsed time and required 10 months' effort.

Aug. 87–Sep. 87
7. Main phase (final cycle)
delivery and club dissolution
This cycle took 2 months and involved very little work from anyone other than the users.

In total the project took 24 months' of elapsed time and required 51 months' of effort.

Fig. 11.6 — The major tasks completed, the knowledge elicitation methods used and the times involved in each cycle.

cycle. The EMEX project is broken up into eight cycles, the majority of the work being performed in cycles 2 to 7 inclusive.

## THE KNOWLEDGE ENGINEERING

The examples of the knowledge engineering documentation presented here constitute only a small proportion generated during the EMEX project. Much of the detailed knowledge engineering documentation is too commercially sensitive to be presented in anything other than the briefest of forms. What is included will provide an illustration of the thought and planning required for interviews, analysis and the work leading towards implementation. Most of the examples are taken from the early cycles in the project. The first fragments of dialogue which appear below are from the structured interview which has been termed interview 1. The agenda for that interview is presented in Fig. 11.11. A detailed questionnaire, derived from the examples in chapter 6 was produced and sent to the expert in advance of the interview. Interview 1 took two sessions of about two hours each. The sessions were held one week apart and involved different experts. This was not a problem as the experts have a high degree of agreement over the basic principles. The differences in opinion were in the areas of detail and emphasis. The analysis of the four hours of audio tape took about 30 hours. This analysis achieved the following documentation set.

## THE KNOWLEDGE ENGINEERING DOCUMENTATION SET

### Selected interview transcripts

These are a combination of word-for-word and paraphrased transcriptions of the salient parts of the interview. An example of the interview transcripts is given below (see Fig. 11.15).

### Preliminary structure of the task

Even with only four hours of interview (plus other unrecorded discussions with the other knowledge engineer) it was possible to draw up the highest level task structure. The boxes in the diagram (Fig. 11.7) where applicable became knowledge-base module for that particular function.

### Future topics list

This is a structured list of matters arising from the first two sessions ordered in terms of whether the topic belongs to the domain or the task, and specifically which area of the domain and task. This document is in a constant state of change.

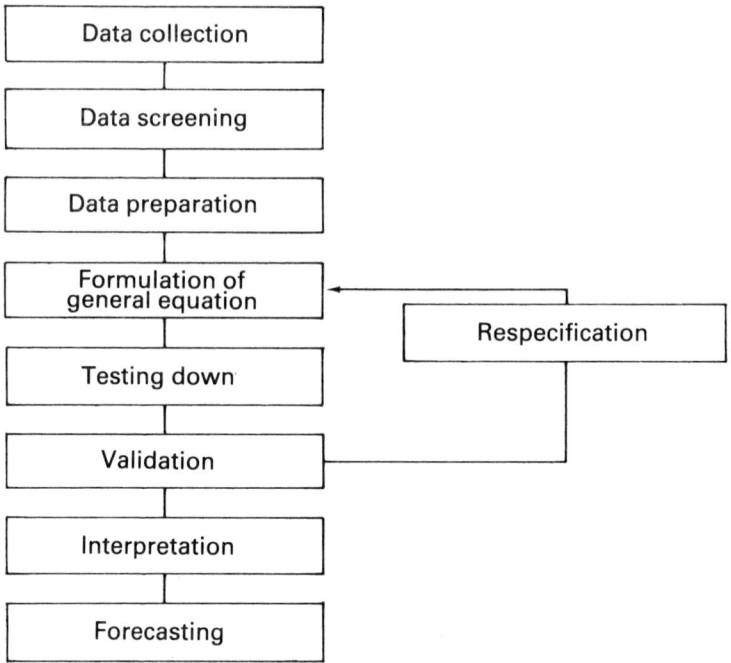

Fig. 11.7 — Structure of econometrics task.

**Domain glossary**
This document falls into two parts. The first part contains all the technical terms used and defined by the expert. The second part contains those terms awaiting full definition or which are still misunderstood.

**Facts list**
A number of unequivocal statements made by the expert.

**Interviews plan**
A plan of the structure of the future interviews with the most immediate being the most detailed. This document avoided problematic subjects being forgotten.

**The agenda for the next interview**
This document was prepared using the previous document, the second part of the domain glossary and future topics list.

**A graphical plan for the next cycle (Fig. 11.8)**
This was produced as a preliminary to a more detailed plan. Although mainly concerned with cycle 3, the plan extends to other cycles.

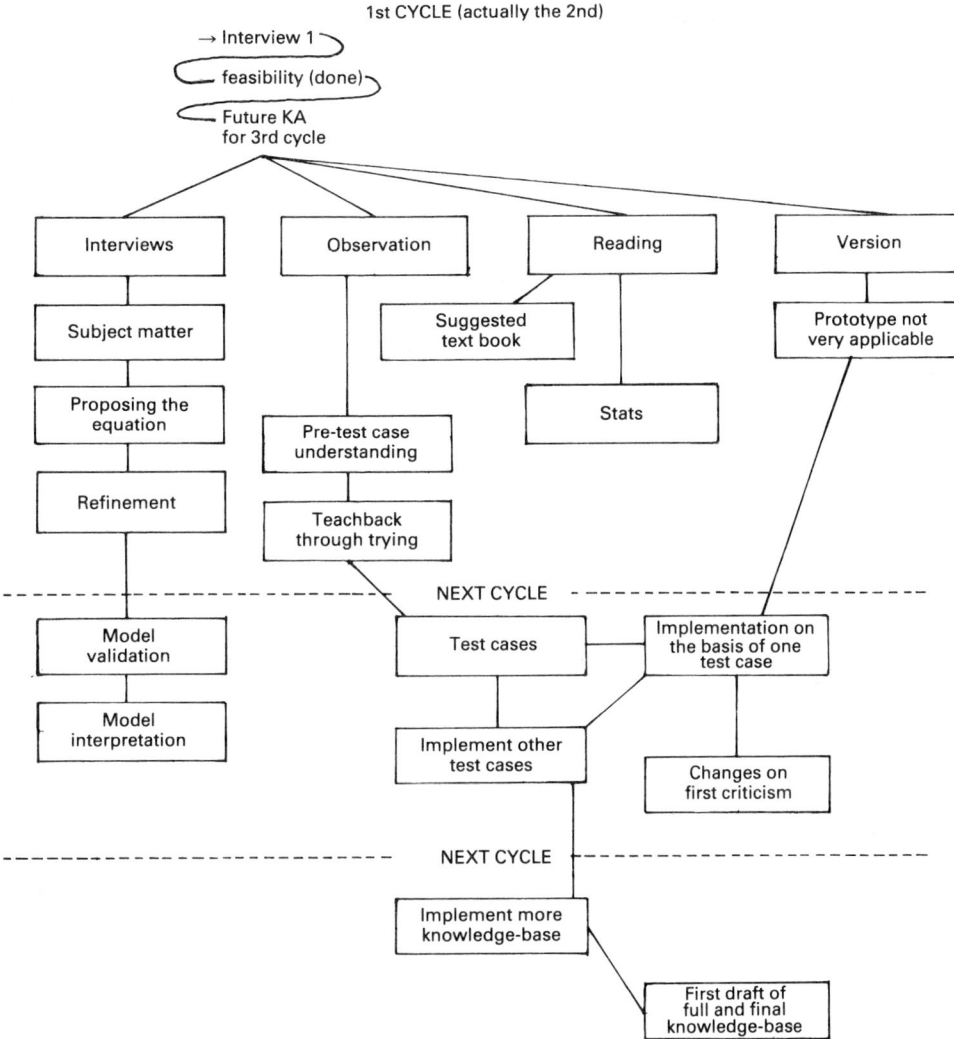

Fig. 11.8 — Knowledge engineering plan for cycle 3.

## A plan of all work including interviews, analysis, design, and early implementation

A computerised project planning system was utilised for this plan and the major points were written up and presented to the steering committee for their agreement.

## A log

General notes made on a daily basis, concerning any aspects of the project mainly knowledge engineering but not exclusively so.

The fact that the feasibility of the project was determined before the author joined the team had little impact on the methodology which was applied to the project. Consequently the knowledge engineering began by defining the principal domain objects and the basic task structure. The decision to represent the domain structure as interlinking frame definitions had already been taken along the lines I would have wished. What had not been finalised was the design of the frame system both in terms of its own internal structure and how it would model the domain. This design was completed immediately following the domain analysis. The designer of the knowledge engineering infrastructure (i.e. the KRL compiler and inference engine) had been involved in some of the early interviews and therefore had a good understanding of the domain and task structure. A by-product of this design process was the formulation of an intermediate representation for the tripartite structure of knowledge and implied in this was the stage of achieving that intermediate representation from the knowledge engineering documentation and my own developing understanding. The tripartite structure of knowledge is diagrammed in Fig. 11.9.

| Level and description | Econometric example | Representation |
|---|---|---|
| 1. Domain: the objects real and imagined manipulated by the expert | Equation Economic factor | Frames |
| 2. Inference: the rules by which values are assigned to the attributes which make up the description of an object | Degrees of freedom of equation =number of observations− number of variables −1. If the returns to scale for a factor are increasing then the representation of that factor is inverse. | uniquely numbered backward and forward chaining rules |
| 3. Task: the procedure by which the expert performs problem solving activity | After a regression remove no more than three variables with $T$-stats lower than 2, choosing the longer lags first | Augmented transition networks divided into task phases |

Fig. 11.9 — The tripartite structure of knowledge.

In designing the frame-based inference shell an incomplete draft of the intermediate representation for the domain structure was produced. This corresponded with further elicitation to increase my understanding of the task. At this point knowledge acquisition superseded elicitation. Whereas elicitation refers solely to the interactions between expert and knowledge engineer, acquisition in this example refers to passive observation, reading text books, analysing artifacts derived from performing the task, to attempting to perform the task.

When the task was understood well enough and the static domain knowledge verified, the detailed analysis of the test cases was undertaken. The most understood, simplistic and successful test case formed the basis of the first attempt at implementation. This working system was then used as a knowledge engineering resource, to be improved and extended following the expert's instructions and criticism. This technique is known as rapid prototyping.

Only when a section of the expert's task was completed to the expert's satisfaction did the knowledge engineer begin the implementation of another area of the expertise. Some of the preliminary work would have already been done on all the areas of expertise during the domain analysis and some overlap between the different areas was achieved by holding interviews with one expert while others were testing the functionality of the up-dated system. But this overlap was slight and the emphasis was always upon getting the current implementation of a section right before concentrating upon the next.

The implementation strategy utilised pencil and paper sketches of the control structure in terms of an augmented transition network. This exactly mirrored the control structure used in the EMEX knowledge representation language. These diagrams were constructed largely from the knowledge engineer's understanding of the procedures carried out by the econometricians with the assistance of draft knowledge-bases (in English) written by the expert. The draft knowledge-bases served a number of functions. Firstly, because of the multi-expert situation in which the overlap of expertise between each expert was so great, and the area of expertise large but modular, the apportionment of describing a particular phase of the task, such as testing down (optimising the general equation by applying a regression technique), or validation, could be given to a single expert. An expert would spend at least one day writing down his or her thoughts on that area of the task. This paper would then be distributed amongst the other experts for comments. Finally, a consensus would be reached and a final draft produced. The resultant booklet was then sent to the club members as a deliverable which was appreciated if not totally understood. This booklet also became a model for the reasoning which underpinned the test cases. Thus, all the test cases had been 'standardised' and where deviations had been necessary a detailed explanation was given. As the draft knowledge-base did not contain the degree of specificity required to write the computer readable knowledge-base I investigated some of the deeper issues with the expert authors. The technique used was the structured interview. The first functioning knowledge-base (after the initial prototype) was the result of the analysis and extension of the English knowledge-base sitting upon the knowledge engineer's understanding and coming from the initial domain analysis. From that point the prototype or version became the principal resource.

The intermediate representation for the task, an augmented transition network, consists of any number of nodes connected by any number of arcs. The structure is quite modular and amenable to any degree of alteration and extension (see Fig. 11.10). If the experts disagreed with the knowledge engineer's interpretation then changes could be made very rapidly and the effects of this change observed after only a short compile time. When an area of knowledge represented by an augmented transition network was suffi-

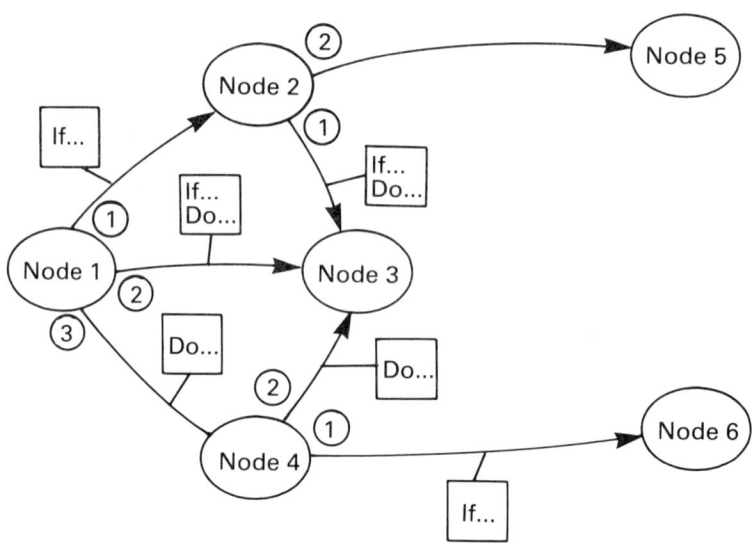

Fig. 11.10 — Simplified view of an Augmented Transition Newtork.

ciently stable the inferencing procedures were transferred where possible from the explicit augmented transition network into the more implicit and mostly backward chaining rules. This had the effect of reducing the size of the knowledge-base and making the results of the inferencing procedures more generally available to any part of the control structure (ATN). The process of transferring the inferential procedures from the ATN to the rules makes the control structure simpler and easier to understand, amend and extend.

Extending the knowledge-base to perform more of the expert's task would usually require an extension of the object (frame) definitions. As these were fairly stable this would usually only involve adding new attributes, some rather obvious default values and rules to infer values for those attributes.

## KNOWLEDGE ELICITATION

The first examples deal with the interviews which were held between M. Greenwell and either Paul Ormroyd or Chris Farmello at the Henley Centre for Forecasting. When I joined the project at the beginning of the first cycle of the main phase, the first prototype had just been released to the club members and a sizable amount of documentation and about fifteen C90 audio cassettes were available for inspection. As an experiment I attempted to utilise these resources to gain an understanding of the domain. However, the knowledge engineering had been carried out in an unstructured manner and was largely oriented towards getting a prototype built rather than developing a deeper understanding or documenting the knowledge in a way which could be easily transferred to another non-expert. Without a structured approach to the knowledge analysis it proved very difficult to achieve the detailed understanding needed for the commencement of the main phase of knowledge engineering. The author was forced to conclude that a modified version of interview 1 should be held after a presentation on expert systems technology.

The agenda for the first interview with the main expert is as in Fig. 11.11.

Interview: 1
Date: 27 June 1986

Agenda
    1. Ascertain domain characteristics
    2. Characterise task
    3. Perform an initial task analysis
    4. Discuss expert's concept of end-user

1.  Ascertain domain characteristics
An orientation to the underlying constructs in the domain. A rough and ready definition of 'domain' is those concepts, theories, models and methodologies that make up the body of knowledge known as econometrics. This is not about doing econometrics but econometrics itself.

2.  Characterise task
These questions deal with the task as an object. I hope to find the task parameters for such things as types of problems and solutions. This is about doing econometrics.

3.  Task analysis
I hope to get a diagrammatic representation of the main problem solving task. This area has already been covered to a large extent.

4.  Discuss expert's concept of the end-user
What is your model of the end user? How do you think we can translate the model building process into a form that will not cause credibility problems for the user who knows little of your expertise.

Fig. 11.11 — Agenda for the first meeting between M Greenwell (KB) and Chris Farmello (EX).

This early interview is concerned with putting the knowledge engineer's understanding on a firm foundation. The interview falls into the category of the structured interview in which the questions are open-ended in order to elicit broad discursive answers. The probes largely deal with covering the subject area at a high level rather than delving into any detailed areas.

Many of the questions that are asked in these interviews have been listed in the section dealing with interview 1. A segment from a recording between the expert and the knowledge engineer illustrates the ease with which information flows in this type of interview.

KE: I'll read this out again just so the tape recorder hears it. Does commonsense knowledge or knowledge from other disciplines or domains have a role in what you do?

EX: At the theoretical level commonsense knowledge has no role whatsoever. However, in practice there is a large input from empiricism and commonsense knowledge. Asking, for example, if the model makes sense. That is economic sense or market specific sense. There is not a lot of commonsense knowledge, but what there is, is important.

KE: Can you give an example?

EX: Common sense is manifested in the form of expectations such as the size of the response.

KE: Response?

EX: The effect of the dependent variable to a known change in one of the independent variables.

KE: Ah! I see.

EX: There are three stages in which common sense makes its presence felt. The first is at the data screening phase. Such as realising that the data is corrupted or will need transforming or massaging in some way before it can be used. Another stage is the testing down phase — do you want me to talk about this yet?

KE: So long as it is not too detailed.

EX: Once again it has to do with expectations. If we were modelling sales against price and if the variable representing price has a positive coefficient, which means when price goes up sales are also going up so when you charge more for something you always sell more, plainly ridiculous, common sense and simple economic theory would suggest something was wrong.

KE: Would this be true in all occasions?

EX: No, there are some goods for which that effect would be expected, but they are very rare and the person building the model would know if the good they were modelling was in that category or not.

KE: I had forgotten that, but from my own limited economics background I believe they are called Giffin goods.

EX: Yes, that's right.

KE: Such things such as bread or potatoes would be consumed more by poor people if the price goes up, that is, in a particular type of economy, and this is because they cannot afford other more expensive food.

EX: Very expensive goods too can fall into this category if a price rise increases demand because of the snob value which is attached.

KE: Can you model these goods?

EX: Oh yes. It's just the response on price would be the opposite to what you would expect on most occasions.

KE: Anything else on common sense?

EX: Yes. The final stage when common sense is useful is when validating the result. I think what I have to say on this is probably too detailed at the moment but has once again to do with expectations and what the model is saying.

KE: That is fine if we just stop there on common sense. What about other

expert knowledge from other domains?
EX: Well, there is economic theory — that is rather basic economics, and of course statistics and that can be rather complex.
KE: So, in order to understand econometrics, do you recommend I refresh my limited statistics knowledge?
EX: Yes.
KE: Perhaps someone from here will tutor me in statistics?
EX: I am sure they will.
KE: I will make overtures to Eric on that one. He said he wanted to be involved and I think that stats is his specialty.

This four or five minutes has provided a lot of useful information. First of all, the limits of commonsense knowledge which has the potential of being problematic has been explored. The issue of the user's expectations seems prominent and this is noted for further investigation and as the most likely method to circumvent and implement common sense.

Basic economics does not appear to be a problem but statistics may well be. What I am interested in is achieving an understanding of the domain before covering the task in detail. In defining the extent and also the requirement for other types of expertise I am able to look for a solution.

Note also that I could not resist the opportunity to show off my limited knowledge. It appears that one of the most contentious statements which has been made in this book concerns the issue of background expertise. That is where the knowledge engineer has a good background in the domain. Some writers appear to think that, rather than being a problem, background knowledge is an asset to such an extent that a knowledge engineer, if naive in the domain, should study text books before meeting the expert (Hart, 1986), and if experienced, should build the prototype before the first contact with the expert. In the dialogue above, my desire to show some of my limited knowledge led me to ask a rather facile question, 'Would this be true on all occasions?' when the answer was already known and when a better probe would have been to investigate what was meant by coefficient. Asking a question when the answer is already known, rather than asking for confirmation to a statement, is, in some cases, a reasonable technique as there may be information which is yet to be discovered. However, the question was asked in order to lead into the discussion that actually took place, which was largely a waste of time. It appears that the knowledge engineer has a psychological need to demonstrate his limited knowledge, which is not his role unless it is part of a validation exercise. Is it true to suggest that the more background knowledge the knowledge engineer has the greater this problem will be?

While analysing the tape I realised these gratuitous expositions of low-level knowledge may become a habit and resolved to use my background knowledge in a constructive manner, but mostly to put it to one side. Nevertheless, readers must decide for themselves whether background knowledge is a benefit or a hindrance to knowledge acquisition.

Even when a question is misunderstood the answer can still provide a lot of useful information. In the next example dialogue, the expert answers the wrong question but the reply is so interesting the knowledge engineer allows the expert to continue before rephrasing the question.

KE: Is it possible to see problems falling into basic types and, if it is, how would you categorise these types, are there a lot of problem types and are these categories prototypical cases?
EX: One problem which is, I think, the most common problem we have to deal with is having too few observations. If this is the case we have a degrees of freedom problem and quite often have to attempt a different method of specific to general.
KE: Hold on there! If I can just jump in here, what does 'degrees of freedom' mean? I used to know, but it is important I get it just right.
EX: Well, as far as the formula goes, that is the number of observations minus the number of variables. However, as to what 'degrees of freedom' means, well, that's different; it's quite succinctly the number of values that a variable is free to vary. If we have 5 sample measurements (uses paper while explaining) — 10, 14, 6, 5 and 5 — these can be represented as deviations from a mean of 8, and so we have 2, 6, −2, −3 and −3. The sum of these is, of course, 0; so if 4 deviations are known, then the remaining deviation is determined. So we say the number of degrees of freedom is 4 in that case. Is that OK?
KE: I think so. I'll read about this too, and talk to Eric if it's still fuzzy.
EX: Now where was I?
KE: Degrees of freedom problem means specific to general.
EX: Ah yes. Otherwise general to specific is used. Many of our problems are market specific and cannot be generalised, and there is a difference between volume and brand share models. It is much more difficult to build a brand share model and again we are back to data that is obtaining data. Companies always underestimate the degree of difficulty in obtaining good data. Because they need data which is beyond their control-data relating to their competitors or data which comes from various departments from within their own organisation — advertising spend is often very difficult to unite with the data relating to sales. New products or new markets have their own special difficulties. I suppose the biggest problem, excepting limited data, is that there is no indication as to the difficulty in building a model before starting. I'm not sure but that may have implications for the expert system.
KE: Perhaps if you explain further.
EX: Well, some models by the very nature of the data contain certain statistical properties which either create spurious models which are statistically correct but have economic abnormalities, or refuse to settle down to a coherent form without some quite complex transformations. Some of these seem — these fixes are quite intuitive.
KE: I see. Yes. There may be problems here. Are models like this common?
EX: No, not really, just unpredictable.
KE: Can — how can I describe them — these deviant models, can they be recognised?

EX: Yes, but I'm not sure I can explain simply how or how easy it is.
KE: Well, there is plenty of time to understand that. Let's get the basics seen to first.
EX: OK. Going back to the difference between brand share and market models — it is not in the techniques used but in the level of practical knowledge used. By 'practical knowledge' I mean experience, recognition of similar situations in the past, things not found in text books, the purposeful forgetting of a significant fact to see if an alternative solution exists . . . .
KE: OK. That's fine. I think you have given me a lot of interesting information there. However, it was in answer to a different question. What I wanted to ask was: is the problem you solve — in a psychological sense — that is the task — are there basic types or categories to that?
EX: Ah, I see. Well, there is market models such as modelling the entire market for cars in the UK, and a brand share model which, let's say, models only Fords or perhaps only one model . . . .

The analysis of such open-ended questions leads to more questions and to more interviews. By progressing in this manner the structured, agenda-orientated interview gradually gives way to the focused, in-depth first interview.

One of the most fruitful forms of knowledge acquisition is the combination of simple (non-participant) observation and focused interviewing. In the last examples of interview dialogue the expert is building a model while I watch and take notes. The expert is sitting at the computer terminal and is using a statistics package. I understand the basic instruction language for this package so the meaning of the expert's commands is quite clear. The expert is explaining what he is doing in quite a discursive manner. The discussion is being recorded and the computer consultation is being logged.

KE: Can you tell me why you're removing that term rather than that one?
EX: Well, with many goods the income effect is short-lived, so I'd look at the longer lags and if they are insignificant I'd remove them. If at this stage especially if the $T$-stat's less than 1 then I'd drop it. Other factors have longer-lasting effects.
KE: That's economic theory?
EX: Er, yes, that's commonsense with economic theory.
KE: Does it depend upon the good?
EX: It's possible — some expensive goods may be more responsive to income changes over a longer time. Comparing new car sales to shoes perhaps; but I generally think income has a short-term effect.

The expert seemed to be breaking one of his own rules so I investigated further. What resulted was a heuristic which was placed in the heuristics document which has steadily been building up during the post-domain analysis phase of the knowledge acquisition.

SITUATION: During testing down.
HEURISTIC: Check longer lags on income terms first.

And more suspect was:

SITUATION: During testing down.
HEURISTIC: The more expensive the good the more lags may be needed on income.

At that time it was unclear if these heuristics will be used, but they should be collected.

The last example dialogue demonstrates the complexities of observing/interviewing/trying to understand at the same time. The situation is the same as the previous example.

KE: I'm lost. What is going on? We did everything right, that is, we followed the book. Is the book wrong?
EX: This is a more common occurrence than you were led to believe.
KE: I was told there would be models like this. OK, let's get this straight. If we were to continue then all we would be left with is the constant, the lagged dependent variable, one rather meaningless differenced term — and those were your words — and the seasonal dummies — not a good model.
EX: Not good at all. Obviously we can't continue down this path.
KE: You said it was bad about three regressions ago, and I didn't believe you. You will have to explain how you knew. We still have a record of that equation so if we . . .
EX: The problem is the data series are interacting in some strange ways. Look, if I do a correlation of these . . . OK, see the high positive correlation there, there and there.
KE: Totally unrelated though. What's it saying?
EX: As that goes up so does that, while that goes down but not so much.
KE: You could have done this at the beginning though.
EX: Indeed I should have done.
KE: So, why not and what can we do? . . . er . . . answer 'why not?' first.
EX: I forgot, and anyway it's worth a try.

This interview carried on in the same vein for quite some time. This was the first time I had seen how the econometrician deals with a very problematic model. The basic rules for constructing models no longer applied and the expert had to constructively solve the problems which were besetting the model using his experience and expertise to the fullest extent. After a time I had to sit back and observe what the expert was doing and leave him to it, knowing I was collecting a detailed record of his interaction with the computer. When the expert considered the task complete, the solution was analysed and a discussion of how that solution was reached ensued. Only after an analysis of the transcript and computer log and another interview with the expert did I begin to realise what he had being doing. Much useful information came from this one session because of the detailed recording of the session.

## INTERMEDIATE REPRESENTATIONS

The effort required to produce the domain glossary should lead directly into an interpretation model of the domain. This is a vital intermediate representation if the implementation is object-oriented or frame-based. An interpretation model (the way I used it may not be the way it was intended by Breuker and Wielinga 1984a) is a form of mental exercise to create a domain hierarchy and therefore to expand one's own understanding of the domain. Everything in the domain can be seen as deriving from the initial inquiry or problem definition. This I have termed as the top level or consultation. The consultation is the name of the top-level object in the KRL which references all the other frames. In fact I found the interpretation model of limited use. There were certain objects which on closer inspection became processes and, thus, more adequately represented by the ATN. However, progress was achieved through mental exercise rather than the use of the model. For the record, the interpretation model for the major objects as pertaining to part of the EMEX system is presented in Fig. 11.12.

As far as I have understood the KADS methodology of Breuker and Wielinga (1984b), the extension of the interpretation model should lead directly into a domain structure. The problem is that there is no consistency as to what formulates a domain structure. The EMEX object definition shown below is specific to the KRL which was written for the project. Many commercial knowledge engineering packages do not offer such a detailed or complex representation as their KADS methodology implies. Its use is limited by the KRL which the knowledge engineer is using. A second restriction on the use of the interpretation model is concerned with the short cuts which are characteristic of all analyses. When you believe you have enough knowledge or an adequate understanding to perform the next step, the present step seems redundant and is usually terminated before completion. The interpretation model will inevitably fall into this category. Unless you find yourself committed to the KADS methodology in full, the use of the interpretation model seems to be limited to segmenting the domain in a coherent fashion from which the knowledge engineer begins the more detailed domain implementation.

## AN EMEX OBJECT DEFINITION

The example of the object which represents the explained factor in the EMEX system is shown in Fig. 11.13. This is an intermediate representation, not the knowledge representation language, although with the addition of a few key words and some syntax it would be a compilable piece of KRL. This representation of the object is used as a shorthand representation of the object's coded definition. The actual code representing both object definition and relevant rules can occupy a great deal of space. However, similar object representations were constructed before implementation.

Fig. 11.13 is an example of how the specification of the objects from the

0PROPOSED OBJECTS — INTERPRETATION MODEL
top level (consultation)
  economic system
    factors
      name
      data frequency
      data source
      explained factor
        inertia
        seasonality statistic
        new product (logistic)
      explanatory factor
        economic category
          income
          price
          advertising [etc.]
        econometric type
          dummy
          seasonal dummy
          economic measure
  equation
    left-hand side
    dependent term
    right-hand side
    constant
    groups
      terms
        lag
        difference
          first
          fourth (or data frequency)
          double
        coefficient
      $T$-statistic
    statistics
      standard error
      Durbin–Watson
      $R$-squared
      sum of squared residuals
    sample period
  user preferences for input
    testing down mode
  processes
    formulation of general equation
    data screening
      trending
      seasonality
      correlations
    testing down
      ordinary least squares regression
      $F$ test
    dropping terms
  validation tests
    Lagrange Multiplier
    Strong Chow
    Weak Chow
    Box–Pierce
    Linearity
    Normality
  interpretation
    seasonal effects
      Box–Jenkins Identification
    dynamic paths
    long run effect

Fig. 11.12 — Interpretation model for the domain of econometrics.

```
EXPLAINED_FACTOR
    is_a factor
        EXPECTED_SEASONAL         24
        INERTIAL                  23
        LOGISTIC                  22
        Q_STAT                    51, 52
        SEASONAL
        (NAME)                    21
        (DATA_SERIES)             8
        (FACTOR_TYPE)             17
        (CATEGORY)                18
        (REPRESENTATION)          240, 241
```

Fig. 11.13.

orientation stage is used as a reference for the model of the system during implementation. The numbers on the right-hand side have been added and relate to the rule numbers which are used to calculate the value for a particular slot. Those slots in brackets are inherited from the parent frame, which in this case is the factor frame.

The last examples, in Fig. 11.14 and 11.15, are of part of the augmented transition network for EMEX and the rules.

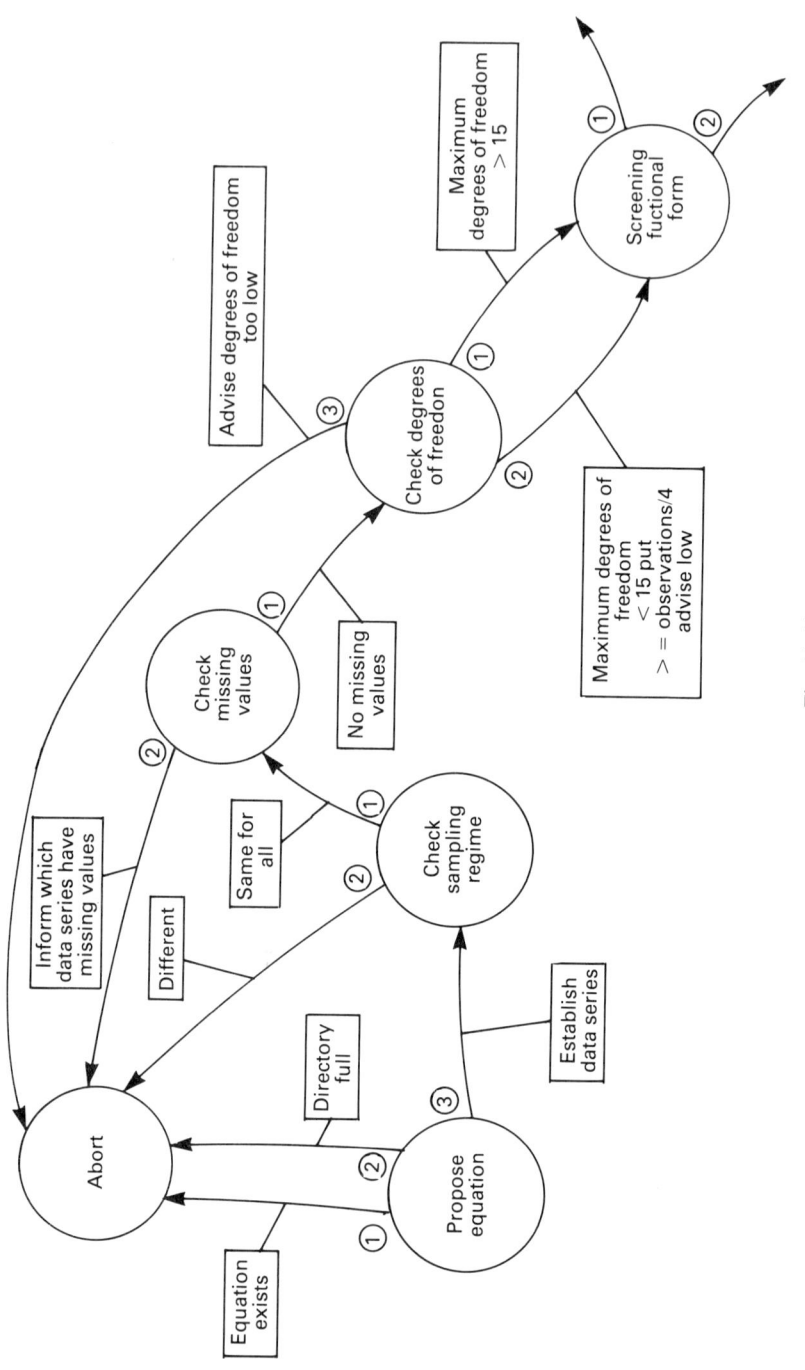

Fig. 11.14.

English: 'price and income would be expected to have a positive coefficient'
29 :: sign_expectation of explanatory_factor
    =positive if
category of explanatory_factor=income or
category of explanatory_factor=price

Fig. 11.15.

# Glossary

Algorithm: A detailed procedure which guarantees a result.

Artificial intelligence: The accademic discipline combining cognitive psychology, philosophy, linguistics and robotics. The aim of which is to simulate and understand intelligent systems by writing computer programs.

Augmented transition network: A control structure which consists of nodes or states, and arcs which traverse the nodes. Control moves across an arc to the next node if a condition is true or if told explicitly to do so. A specific arc may detail a number of actions which must be performed before arriving at the next node.

Backward chaining: The inferencing strategy by which a result or conclusion is found by ascertaining whether the conditions which support the conclusion is true. In attempting to find the value of the conclusions more backward chaining may result which means the whole process can be very complicated but each backward chaining rule can be quite simple and internally meaningful.

Cognition: The inferred information processes which account for mental phenomena such as memory, perception, problem solving or any other mental behaviour.

Forward chaining: The inferencing strategy by which a rule is triggered by an event such as an addition of information to the system. Events may be caused as the result of other rules being triggered.

Frames: A complex data structure which represents a description of an object, either real or imagined. A frame consists of a title and a number of slots which represent those attributes which describe the object. Frames should also contain specific links to other frames and methods by which instances of a frame can be created. A frame is a stereotypical representation of an object which may pass on some or all of this information to other frames which are said to inherit that information.

Econometrics: The application of statistical techniques to discover systematic and quantified relationships between movements in one variable, such as sales, and movements in a number of other variables, such as prices, advertising, after-tax incomes and so on.

Expert system: A computer system that either simulates the behaviour of a recognised human expert or provides a service which is recognised to be of the same standard as a human expert, should one exist to perform a similar task.

Heuristic: A rule of thumb. A piece of knowledge which is useful some or most of the time but the application of which does not always guarantee success.

KADS: Knowledge Acquisition Documentation System, a computer program/methodology which has emerged from the University of Amsterdam over recent years.

Knowledge acquisition: The process by which knowledge is gathered, from whatever source, to be represented within an Expert System.

Knowledge-base: The systematic, structured representation of the domain knowledge in a source suitable for the computer.

Knowledge engineer: The individual who builds all or part of an expert system.

Knowledge engineering: The process of building expert systems including identification, feasibility, knowledge acquisition, knowledge analysis, implementation, delivery and maintenance.

Knowledge elicitation: The process of obtaining information from a recognised expert, usually by interviews or forms of observation.

Knowledge representation language: A high level computer language capable of representing the acquired domain knowledge.

Production rule: The most simplistic form of knowledge representation, which generally reads as a conditional statement: if X then Y, where X is usually a collection of predicates joined by logical connectives, 'or', 'and' and 'not'.

Script: A control structure which represents a typical sequence of events.

Shell: A computer program which manipulates the knowledge-base, drawing conclusions from the data which is provided. Most shells are based on a simple production rule strategy. They have little or no flexibility as to what inference strategies can be used and cannot allow changes in the interface.

Toolkit: An expert systems toolkit provides low level and high level constructs so that knowledge engineers can determine their own reasoning strategies, knowledge representation language and user interface.

# Bibliography

Lisanne Bainbridge: Asking Questions and Accessing Knowledge. *Future Computing Systems* **1**, (2), 143–149 (1986).

A well written concise paper which unfortunately just scrapes the surface of a major issue: What methods are best suited to what situations? Even so the conclusions are well worth taking on board as guidelines to the choice of method.

Annabel C. Beerel: *Expert Systems: Strategic Implications and Applications*. Ellis Horwood, Chichester (1987).

Ms Beerel has a strong business and management background. This means she says a lot of sensible things about business but is rather confused when it comes to expert systems. This is evident by the concentration upon knowledge, which is always fruitless, and the gratuitous name-dropping (Piaget, J. S. Mills, Descartes, etc.). One chapter dealing with the socio-technical issues is good and was what I hoped the book would concentrate upon. In conclusion, it seems the book's ideal role is to initiate ideas rather than supply them.

Joost, A., Breuker and Bob J. Wielinga: Analysis Techniques for Knowledge Based Systems Part 1, Report 1.1 Esprit Project 12 Memorandum 10 of the Research Project 'The Acquisition of Expertise'. University of Amsterdam, Department of Social Science Informatics and Laboratory for Experimental Psychology, Weesperplein 8, 1018 XA Amsterdam, October (1983a).

Joost, A. Breuker and Bob J. Wielinga: Analysis Techniques for Knowledge Based Systems Part 2, Report 1.2, Esprit Project 12 Memorandum 12 of the Research Project 'The Acquisition of Expertise'. (See above) December (1983b).

Joost A. Breuker and Bob J. Wielinga: Interpretation of Verbal Data for Knowledge Acquisition, Report 1.4 Espirit Project 12 Memorandum 27 of the Research Project 'The Acquisition of Expertise'. (See above) June (1984a).

Joost, A., Breuker and Bob J. Wielinga: Techniques for Knowledge Elcitation and Analysis, Report 1.5 Project 12 Memorandum 28 of the Research Project 'The Acquisition of Expertise'. (See above) July (1984b).

Breuker and Wielinga have sketched out the boundaries to the domain of knowledge acquisition. Their work is a development of that originally done by Grover and Clancey, which moves knowledge acquisition towards a more practical perspective. Unfortunately their reports do not make for easy reading, and the development of the KADS methodology appears somewhat esoteric.

H. M. Collins, R. H. Green and R. C. Draper: Where's the Expertise: Expert Systems as a Medium of Knowledge Transfer. *Expert Systems 85, Proceedings of the Fifth Technical Conference of the British Computer Society*, Specialist Group on Expert Systems, (ed. Martin Merry), 323–334 (1985).

This article has important, if not fundamental, implications for knowledge acquisition. It should be compulsory reading for all would-be knowledge engineers. The problems of tacit knowledge which they describe probably constitute the major stumbling block to the greater acceptance of expert systems as a reliable software solution.

Mark D. Grover: *A Pragmatic Knowledge Acquisition Methodology*, pp. 436–438. Proceedings of IJCAJ-8 (1983).

Anna Hart: *Knowledge Acquisition for Expert Systems*. Kogan Page, London (1986).

The first attempt at exploring the knowledge acquisition domain in a book form. It seems rather obvious that the author has not worked on a realistic application and this devalues the book as a practical guide to expert systems.

F. Hayes-Roth, D. A. Waterman and D. B. Lenat (eds): *Building Expert Systems*. Addison-Wesley, Reading, Massachusetts (1983).

This book tells you all you need to know about building expert systems, apart from how to do it. Still, I found chapter 5 to be a good read even though the rest was pretty unimpressive.

E. T. Keravnou and L. Johnson: *Competent Expert Systems*. Kogan Page, London (1986).

The first few chapters of this book are excellent, if not particularly easy to read. The book takes an implementation perspective, which is appreciated in view of the large number of speculative academic texts which have flooded the book shelves. If anything, their book is spoilt by over-indulgence in the details of, 'our expert system', which is about as interesting as other people's dreams.

Philip E. Slatter: *Building Expert Systems: Cognitive Emulation.* Ellis Horwood, Chichester (1987).

Cognitive emulation is concerned with duplicating the expert's actual reasoning processes. Experts may perform sophisticated pattern matching rather than problem solving; this learned cognitive style separates the experts from the learners. As a design guideline, cognitive emulation has a lot going for it. Slatter's book presents a balanced view as to the pros and cons for using this approach and generally comes out on the side of the pros.

M. Wellbank: A Review of Knowledge Acquisition Techniques for Expert Systems, Memorandum No. R19/022/83. British Telecom Research Laboratories, Martlesham Heath Ipswich IP5 7RE, November (1983).

One of the first reviews of the literature in the field. It is a little out of date now, but has provided a starting point for many knowledge engineers and authors on the subject.

Sylvie Barthelemy, Goran Edin, Emmanuel Toutain and Steven Becker: Requirements Analysis in KBS Development, ESPRIT *1098, A methodology for knowledge-based systems,* Cap Sogeti Innovation S.A.

Brouwer-Janse and Pitt: *Knowledge Acquisition: Methodological Issues and Problem Solving Profiles,* Proceedings of ECAI, Vol. 2, pp. 120–127 (1986).

G. A. Kelly: *The Psychology of Personal Constructs,* Norton, New York (1955).

K. L. McGraw and M. R. Seale: Knowledge elicitation with multiple experts, *AI Review,* **2,** No. 1 (1988).

J. Regan: Expert's categories, Paper given at the Fringes section of the BCS Conference on Expert Systems (1986).

P. Slater: Contrasting correlates of group size, *Sociometry,* **25,** 1229–1239 (1958).

I. Steiner: *Group Process and Productivity,* Academic Press, New York (1972).

S. Wood: Expert systems for theoretically ill-formulated domains, Proceedings of BCS Conference on Expert Systems (1986).

# Index

agenda, 46, 100
agenda for next interview, 160
agenda for first meeting between KE and EX, 165
algorithmic solution, 143
alternative solutions, 121
ALVEY, 150
analysis, 16
analytical behaviour elicitation, 61
analytical techniques analysis book, 97
answers, 34
antecedents, 36
assessment, 136
assessment and evaluation, 147
augmented transition networks, 162
automatic elicitation, 13

background expertise, 107
Bainbridge, 71
Barthelomy *et al.*, 65
behavioural components of expertise, 17
bias, 36, 71
brain storming, 65, 66
Breuker and Wielinga, 47, 49, 111
Brouwer-Janse and Pitt, 108

chicken soup, 28
clients, questions for, 130
clients understanding of expertise, 88
coaching systems, 13, 77, 89
cognitive processing, 16
cognitive psychology, 11, 51
Collins *et al.*, 28
competing domain theories, 79
complexity limit, 143
conversation, 24
cost, 121
creativity, 16
critical response method, 53
cycle of tasks on the EMEX project, 155

data, ambiguous or misleading, 84
data, form of, 84
data, interpretation, 84
data, reliability, 84
decision analysis book, 97
decision support system, 12, 77
defining the problem, 83
Derived knowledge book, 91
decriptive formalisms of the domain, 81
decision elicitation, 60
documentation set, 95
domain analysis for multiple experts, 64
domain complexity, 80
domain documentation, 81
domain glossary, 160
domain knowledge, changing, 81
domain knowledge, reliability, 81
domain objects, structure of, 59
domain specific vocabulary, 34

EMEX, 150
EMEX characteristics of the project, 152
EMEX membership, 151
EMEX object definition, 171
EMEX project expenditure, 156
expectations, 120
expert disagreement, 80
expert participation, 90
expert research, 84
expert synthesis system, 63
expert's interaction with client, 88
expert's roles in the organisation, 90
expert system, reasons for, 123
expert task, advice of others, 86
expert task, backtracking, 86
expert task, complications, 85
expert task, constraints of, 85
expert task, creative components, 86
expert task, media of, 84
expert task, no solution to the, 83
expert task, problems or errors, 85
expert task, stages of, 83

expert task, standard routines, 85
expert task, time taken, 83
expert task, types of, 82
expert task, types of solutions, 83
epistemic net, 105
explanations, 89

facts book, 96
feasibility, 26, 141
feasibility for multiple expert projects, 64
feasibility, managerial, 129
feasibility report, 94, 124
feasibility report for EMEX, 151
feasibility study, 48, 120
feasibility, technical, 128
first cut phase, 142
first cut phase, tasks for, 144
first cut phase, EMEX project, 154
focused interview, 47
forward scenario simulation, 57
frames, 112
future topics list, 158
fuzzy knowledge, 80

glossary, 96
goal decomposition, 58
group elicitation methods, 66

Hart, 44, 56
help system, 89

information processing strategies, 110
information processing strategies with relevant primitive operations, 111
initial findings, 141
initial plan, 92
inquisitive observation, 58
intermediate representations, 103, 171
interpretation model, 171, 172
interpretation model technique, 111
'interview 1', 48, 76, 93, 120
interview analysis, 98
interview, duration of, 47
interview pace, 37
interview plan, 160
interview setting, 38
interview, structure of, 46, 48
interview transcription, 98
interview transcripts book, 96

jargon, 34
judgemental behaviour, 81

KADS methodology, 171
Kelly, 55
Keravnou and Johnson, 105

knowledge acquisition, definition of, 11
knowledge acquisition methodology, 22
knowledge acquisition plan, 97
knowledge analysis, 103, 125, 139
knowledge analysis checklist, 126
knowledge-base, 50
knowledge-based information system, 12, 77
knowledge czar, 64
knowledge elicitation, definition of, 11
knowledge elicitation, eight major areas of, 93
knowledge engineer, roles of the, 45
knowledge engineering benefits, 123
knowledge engineering documentation set, 158
knowledge engineering plan, 99, 161
knowledge engineering report, 141
knowledge external to the domain, role of, 80

main phase, EMEX, 155
management checklist, 129
management methodology, 135
McGraw and Seale, 66
mental and behavioural components of expertise, 19
mental states continuum, 17
motivation, 32
multiple experts, 63, 163

nominal group technique, 67

object structure for wine making, 114
opinion poll, 25
optimising the techniques, 70
orientation phase, 46

participation, 31
personnel, EMEX project, 156
phases of an expert system project, 93
planning and preparation, 92
planning the next interview, 100
police interrogation, 25
preliminary phase, 141, 151
preliminary structure of the task, 158
primitive problem solving operations, 110
primitives inventory, 96
probe, addition, 50
probe, change of mode, 51
probe, defining, 51
probe, directive, 51
probe, reflecting, 50
problem solving systems, 13, 77
procedural behaviour, 16
production rules, 108
project cycles, 136
project log, 99
prototype, 69

psychological inteview, 24

questions, closed, 34
questions for interview 1, 78
questions for interview 1, the environment, 86
questions for interview 1, the expert, 89
questions for interview 1, the modality, 87
questions for interview 1, the task, 81
questions for interview 1, the user, 88
questions, leading, 36
questions, non directional, 34
questions, open, 35

rapid prototyping, 163
rational task description, 96
repertory grids, 54
report by commentary, 54
requirements analysis, 65
relational networks, 106
review, 33
review, 61
rules, backward chaining, 162
rules, forward chaining, 162

second level preparation, 101
selected interview transcripts, 158
self report, 51
shells, expert system, 52
Shaw and Gaines, 55, 57
Slater, 66
social knowledge, 16
software, 118
specification, 125
status transition diagram, 106
statement of requirements, 139, 142

Steiner, 66
stimulus materials, 69
strategic implications, 131
strategic issues, 120
structrue of econometrics task, 160
structured English, 105
structured interviewing, 49
systematic symptom to fault links, 60
systems analysis, 25, 121

tacit knowledge, 28
task analysis, 40
task analysis tree, 108
task breakdown for the cycle, 140
task structure, 119
tasks to be achieved throughout the project, 118
teachback, 33, 62
technical feasibility checklist, 128
test case analysis book, 97
test cases, 53, 66, 69, 70, 140
test cases for multiple experts project, 66
text books, use of, 45
theoretical status of the domain, 79
think aloud protocols, 81, 108
three areas of software, 145
translator, 63
training procedures, 90
tripartite structure of knowledge, 162
two way design pressures, 143

user, the, 38, 65, 88, 94, 130, 141
user analysis, 38, 41
user analysis checklist, 137

Wood, 54

**DATE DUE**